COST-EFFECTIVE

Child Custody

LITIGATION

Samuel E. Thomas and Kumudha N. Kumarachandran

AMERICAN BAR ASSOCIATION
Family Law Section

Cover design by ABA Design

Printed in the United States of America.

26 25 24 23 22 5 4 3 2 1

Library of Congress Control Number: 2022903666

ISBN: 9781639051168; e-ISBN: 9781639051175

Discounts are available for books ordered in bulk. Special consideration is given to state bars, CLE programs, and other bar-related organizations. Inquire at Book Publishing, ABA Publishing, American Bar Association, 321 N. Clark Street, Chicago, Illinois 60654-7598.

www.shopABA.org

To my late parents.
You taught me many life lessons I still use in
the practice of law.
I love and miss you both.
—Samuel E. Thomas

To my mother, my colleagues, and most of all, my clients.
—Kumudha N. Kumarachandran

Contents

Acknowledgments vii
About the Authors ix

Chapter 1 Introduction and Initial Tips.......... 1

Chapter 2 Alternative Billing Models for Attorney Representation.......... 9

Chapter 3 Must-Have Technology to Effectively Represent and Expedite (and Make Your Life Simpler).......... 21

Chapter 4 Use No- and/or Low-Cost Methods for Factual Development 33

Chapter 5 Discovery and How to Effectively Get Your Needed Evidence 47

Chapter 6 Dealing with the Unrepresented Opposing Party 57

Chapter 7 Explore and Develop Options for Finding Low-Cost (Necessary) Professionals 63

Chapter 8 Techniques for Settling at Mediation.......... 75

Chapter 9 **To Depose or Not to Depose** **81**

Chapter 10 **The Cost-Effective Trial** **87**

Chapter 11 **Litigating Child Custody in a Pandemic** **97**

Chapter 12 **Final Points** **103**

Appendix 1: Sample Engagement Letter for Contested Child Custody Matter 106

Appendix 2: Commonly Requested Documents List in Child Custody Litigation 109

Appendix 3: Child Custody Case Intake Form 110

Appendix 4: Subpoena for Production of Documents 115

Appendix 5: Child Custody Interrogatories 118

Appendix 6: Request for Production of Documents for Child Custody Cases 120

Index 127

Acknowledgments

This book was not written alone. This book comes from years of representing clients with low to no means of payment. I quickly learned that to be the lawyer required of my clients, I had to be creative, resourceful, and work smarter and harder than my opponent.

I also have to thank the many attorneys I have learned from in my career in my local area as well as the great lawyers who are members of my family in the American Bar Association (ABA) Family Law Section. Your expertise has made the drafting of the ideas and material in this book much simpler. I cannot thank all of you, but I would like to thank a few of the people who particularly informed my knowledge of child custody litigation. Chaim Steinberger has provided insight in many child custody topics in the ABA Family Law Section as well as producing a CLE at the 2019 ABA Family Law Section Fall Conference in Austin, Texas. I'd also like to thank Sarah White from the Atlanta Legal Aid for her collaboration for a CLE, and Brook Whitley for helping edit the content. I'd like to thank my mentors out of law school, John Timmons and the late John Kupris, who gave me amazing mentoring on how to be the lawyer I needed to become in my career. Lastly, I'd like to thank my family, both the ones who are here and the ones that I have lost. Without them, I am not the person I am today. I hope this book lives up to your expectations.

—Samuel E. Thomas

To my co-author, Sam, thank you for putting your faith in me and allowing me to join in on this brainchild of yours. This has truly been a passion project. The financial impact of litigation on my clients and their children is always on my mind as I practice. In sharing these cost-effective strategies, I hope to help those of you who feel the same. I would like to thank our family in the ABA Family Law Section as well. While there are far too many to name, the Section has brought me so many people who have helped without hesitation, believed in me, and shaped me into the lawyer I am today. A special thank-you goes out to my work family; I am eternally grateful for your constant support and leadership. Finally, I would like to thank my friends and family for their endless love and encouragement.

—Kumudha N. Kumarachandran

About the Authors

Samuel E. Thomas is an attorney specializing in Family and Immigration Law in Athens, Georgia. He has been named "Online Athens Best of the Best" and "Flagpole Magazine's Athens Favorites" multiple years. In 2021, he was named a *Super Lawyers Rising Star*. Sam is a graduate of the University of Georgia (B.A. in Political Science) and the University of Alabama School of Law. He is licensed to practice law in all courts in Georgia and Tennessee. Sam also serves many roles in different committees within the ABA Family Law Section. In his free time, he loves reading, traveling, watching and playing sports, and spending time with his wife Tonya, son Richard, and their two dogs.

Kumudha N. Kumarachandran is a family law attorney practicing in Baltimore, Maryland. Kumudha received her BA in Government and Politics from the University of Maryland and her JD from the University of Baltimore. For six consecutive years, Kumudha has been named a *Super Lawyers Rising Star*. In 2020, she received the *Maryland Daily Record*'s "Leadership in Law" award and in 2021 was named to their "VIP List—Very Important Professionals Successful by 40." Kumudha first joined the ABA Family Law Section as a fellow from 2015 through 2017 and has continued to hold various committee leadership roles since then. She is a fellow of the American Bar Foundation and a former fellow of the Maryland State Bar Association's Leadership Academy. Outside of work, she enjoys oil painting and spending time with her dog, Maddie.

About the Authors

1

Introduction and Initial Tips

Lawyers represent many clients who come from modest means. This is not always a choice, but it is a reality in many places where law is practiced. Lawyers who know this reality must use resources that are low to no cost to effectively represent their clients in contested family law matters. However, the authors have found that the tips and resources available for family law attorneys are severely lacking, particularly for clients of modest means. Our hope is that this book can be a true resource for those lawyers battling in the trenches daily who find themselves in situations like these.

Whether you are trying to represent family or friends with little income, are trying out child custody litigation as a new field, or representing child custody clients in the rural areas of America, you need cost-saving tips to help zealously advocate for your clients. The tips in this book can help you accomplish that goal. The material is broken into a chronological timeline of a typical contested family law case. Throughout the chronological timeline, quick "*Cost Savings Tips*" are offered that you can employ in your practice. Prior to digging right into the timeline, however, some preliminary tips are presented that could be of assistance to your practice from the initial consultation to the moment you file your petition.

SET THE TONE EARLY AND OFTEN

As most of us know, clients who are in our offices for a child custody dispute are oftentimes as emotional as divorcing clients. We are about to assist them with the one part of their life that is most personal to them, their children. How we approach such a situation in the client's life will often determine how many phone calls and headaches we will receive during this litigation. So how can we better manage the client's expectations and fears from the beginning?

The first consultation with the client is where this process begins. You want the client speaking openly about their entire custody matter while getting the pertinent information for your initial pleadings and case theme. Try to give the client the impression that it is a relaxing atmosphere in your office. Attempt to be more of the "counselor" at law rather than the attorney. Choose warm colors (yellows, tan, etc.) to present a "safe" space where the client can truly open up. Use a softer tone in your voice. Ask them open-ended questions to get them expressing their concerns. Client after client will land in an office after having consultations with other lawyers who have yelled at them, cut them off in the middle of their story, belittled them, and pushed the issue of money immediately at the beginning. They are often shocked during their consultations to find themselves in an office that cares.

Once the client has chosen to hire you and the engagement letter has been signed, shift to the business/attorney side of the transaction. This is where the first expectation can be set forth to the client.

Psychological Counseling

Clients and attorneys alike should be aware of the emotional stages of separating and divorcing. The initial phase of deciding to end the relationship is wrought with contention and destructive behavior. It is followed by a painful emotional transition from being a couple to being a well-adjusted single person. During that transition is when we see the more unsettling behavior from the client. The transition is complete when they are able to emotionally support themselves and take action, without the influence of the other party. By knowing where the client is emotionally, you can help gauge their ability to come to an agreement.[1] If they are blinded by anger or resentment, it can be hard to get them to think about what is best for their kids versus what will most hurt their ex. By helping them get the resources they need to get through the transition, you are helping them put their kids first.

One of the first paragraphs of a good engagement letter should be the *Psychological/Counseling* provision. This is included here should you wish to employ its use:

> If you are not in counseling, we highly recommend that you consider it. The length and expense of your case is usually affected by the intensity of the parents' feelings. During a child custody matter, many people experience emotions that are difficult to handle without professional help. We find that the money invested in psychological help is well spent because the client is better able to cope with the stress of the case. Counseling often results in reduced attorneys' fees and length of litigation.

Always ask if the client is currently involved in counseling. Create a "cheat sheet" of counselors in your local area who you have known clients to have success with in family law issues. Offer the counselor's names to the clients should they want them. Stress that you are not requiring it but that counselors can handle problems with which you have no expertise. Clients have usually welcomed this suggestion, and many are able to differentiate a legal problem from an emotional one they are experiencing. Further explain to the client, and be hopeful that they process it, that it is better to speak with their counselor instead of reacting to an ugly text message from the other parent. The counselor may be able to diffuse the situation and have the client understand that the ugly message may have been misinterpreted.

You can also provide your contact information to the counselor your client wishes to use. This person can contact your office and/or cell phone should the need arise or if the counselor may feel your expertise is better suited for the client's issue. The counselor usually respects the attorney's time and will not keep you on the phone for longer than needed.

---

[1] Robert B. Moriarty, *Using a Resource Counselor*, in 101+ Practical Solutions For The Family Lawyer: Sensible Answers To Common Problems 17 (Gregg Herman ed., 2009).

Cost Saving Tip: Some firms choose to use a resource counselor to refer clients to the specific services they need. A resource counselor is not an employee of the firm; rather, they are someone you can connect your client with. A resource counselor speaks with the client to assess their needs and concerns, then acts as a liaison to connect them with the services of others—be they therapists, support groups, or community agencies.[2]

Goals

Another approach you can take with a new child custody client to start the representation on the right foot is to simply ask: "What are your goals with this matter?" Carefully listen to their response. Write it down. Repeat it back to the client as a question; for example, "Am I clear that your goals here are to . . . .?" The client may run to your office under the initial goal of wanting full custody of all children they have by their former partner. However, you may learn that they want to add a couple more days a month to their parenting time, the result, in this scenario, being much less litigation and months of discovery and depositions not being required. Asking about the client's goals also could help rule out things you simply cannot obtain in the litigation. An example of this would be a client attempting to acquire the dependency credits under federal taxes without obtaining primary physical custody.

Right of Withdrawal

In the engagement contract, consider laying out the circumstances under which you reserve the right to withdraw from the representation of the client, outside of payment-related issues. This is crucial in modest means and pro bono-type cases. You may never have to invoke this provision—indeed, we hope you will not—but it cannot hurt to remind the client that they, too, have obligations in your relationship.

[2] Geoffrey Hamilton & Thomas S. Merrill, *What Happens Emotionally in a Divorce and Why You Should Care and How Do You Know How Your Client Is Faring During the Divorce Litigation?*, *in* 101+ Practical Solutions For The Family Lawyer: Sensible Answers To Common Problems 17 (Gregg Herman ed., 2009).

As a sample language provision, here is a section of the retainer agreement used by the Atlanta Legal Aid Society:

> Legal Aid may stop representing me if I do not cooperate fully and promptly, if Legal Aid determines my case does not have enough legal basis or is not likely to provide substantial benefit for me, if I misrepresent or fail to disclose material facts, or if I become ineligible for Legal Aid's services. In addition, there may be other reasons that Legal Aid may withdraw from representing me. I may fire Legal Aid at any time for any reason.
>
> I agree not to settle my case without Legal Aid's approval. If I reject a settlement offer that Legal Aid recommends to me, Legal Aid may withdraw from my case.

Always point this section out to clients, since it is most effective where the client has actual knowledge and understanding of it. The language about settlement is key in family law cases, especially where attorneys may put in considerable time and effort in crafting a settlement that resolves all the issues, only to have a client reject it based on negative feelings about the other party.

This paragraph further cements the goals you have established (see the prior section) and serves as a reminder that if partial or full settlement is available, it is usually a better and more certain way of reaching those goals than a contested trial. Finally, if you do have to employ this section, always keep in mind that you may have ethical duties to the client that will prevent attorney withdrawal even where permitted by the retainer. Check the ethics opinions and rules in your local jurisdiction for proper withdrawal.

The Client's Story

At the conclusion of an initial hiring, give the client multiple "homework" assignments. Among these assignments are completion of the mandatory financial disclosure affidavit, crafting a proposed parenting time plan the client would like to have in this case, and providing a list of documents commonly requested in a family law matter (see Appendix). Ask the client to write their "story." Simply tell them to go home, pull out Microsoft Word, and tell you the story from the moment they met the other parent and type all events until the present date. The typical number of pages will vary from client to client. The idea here is to get them to flush out all details of their life as it relates to the relationship, the birth of the child(ren) in this matter, and the involvement of each parent as it relates to the daily life of the child(ren). The utility of this document will be incomparable as you are preparing for a temporary hearing in the matter. When you read the story of the client, your direct examination will essentially write itself. It will further give your thoughts for cross examination of the other side. Lastly, it will sometimes provide the "theme" you need to tell the story to the court in a hearing. Reread this document multiple times the night prior to the hearing to gain insight into the client's state of mind so you can better tell their story to the court.

Request Pictures of the Client's Home

Feeding off the story requested above, remember a picture is worth a thousand words. Have your client take pictures of their home. Have them take pictures of the kitchen, the child(ren)'s bedroom, living room, backyard, apartment complex playground, etc. to show the judge in the case of where the child will be living if your client retains or obtains custody. It should be common sense, but have the client CLEAN the home prior to taking pictures. It is also helpful to have the pictures appear natural rather than staged. The judge will always appreciate the visuals rather than having your client simply describe the layout of their home and how the child's bedroom looks.

Using the Client as "The Runner"

Often, you can use the client as the person to go get the documents needed for the prosecution of their child custody case. If you need a police report, for instance, you can send the client to acquire it. The client then feels involved in their own litigation, and they appreciate saving money by not being billed for tasks they can complete themselves. If it is any type of business record, make sure you give them a copy of a blank records certification for the custodian to sign off on.

> ***Cost Saving Tip*: Medical facilities will often charge an attorney to get medical records/bills but do not charge the parent/client for the same records. Send the client instead!**

Come Up with a "Plan" and Stick to It

A helpful tool that has worked for many lawyers with child custody litigation after acquiring the client's "goals" above is to work up a "plan." This lets your client know that you understand what they are seeking and have a map to tackle these goals. Too often attorneys tackle the client's goals and the client is left wondering exactly what you are doing for them. An example of one goal in your multistep plan would be where your client wants a Guardian Ad Litem to represent the children in the custody litigation. Tell them you are going to file a *Motion to Appoint a Guardian Ad Litem.* Allow the client to review the *Motion* via their client portal (discussed in chapter 3). Ask for their approval to file it. The client sees you are working on their case and protecting their rights, and they will appreciate your efforts, the result being, most times, that the client does not call as frequently asking for updates.

Meeting Questions

Another item that clients should use in their interactions with you and your representation is prepared questions. If the client is sitting at home, they can calmly and thoroughly write down the questions they have about their case, tactics, etc. If they are sitting at your desk without a list, rest assured they have not asked all their questions. Too often, follow-up emails are sent within one hour after the meeting asking multiple questions they forgot while sitting in your office.

Responsiveness of the Client

In any practice today, you should strive to be a tech-savvy attorney. The result is that clients are expected to use their client portal regularly and/or check their email daily. This is usually easier given the tech age we live in. However, sometimes we as lawyers represent elder grandparents who are seeking custody and they may not be as adept with technology as younger clients. Tell your clients to please check their email frequently to make sure they miss no communication with your office and/or the other side. Client case management software should always alert the client by email when something has been added to their electronic case file. With clients who do not use technology (rarer today), you may need to take the additional step and call or text them to give them the update. The idea is that if you receive something from opposing counsel, you need a response from your client so you know what they wish the next step to be, given the new information.

CONCLUSION

These tips above should get you and the client on the same page at the initial consultation. The idea is to set the tone that the client is very active in their own case while you set the expectations you have of them. They should walk away from your office knowing exactly what the next step is and what your plan of attack is. Using the tips should lead to better client relations as the litigation progresses.

2

Alternative Billing Models for Attorney Representation

Abraham Lincoln once explained, "a lawyer's time and advice are his stock in trade." In other words, we bill for our time! We need to be clear from the start what exactly we are going to bill the client for. Clarify with the client regarding what you bill for so that you do not have a bill dispute later on with your client and/or your state bar. It is good to emphasize from the outset that they will be billed for telephone calls, emails, and all correspondence, not just between the two of you, but also between you and the other side as well as third parties. This is one of the most common first-bill gripes from clients—that they didn't know they were being billed for communications. It is also good to emphasize this point, so that you don't get thrown into the role of therapist from the beginning. Clients might think your fees are just for writing, or just for court appearances, or they might have other misconceptions about billing if they never hired a lawyer before. Unlike other types of law, family law cases often involve people who have never had to hire a lawyer before. Our litigants are just everyday people who decided to have kids with someone they no longer agree with.

With regard to additional costs, the next portion of your engagement letter has been created to help spell it out for the client to consider:

> *In addition to the attorney rates described above, you also will pay out-of-pocket costs incurred in your case. Typical costs incurred are: photocopies, postage, word processing, long-distance telephone calls and faxes, computer research time, process servers, court filing fees, court reporters, witness fees, out-of-town travel, experts, and investigators. We will not hire any experts and/or investigators unless you agree that they should be hired. You will pay directly for their services.*

This list is, of course, not exhaustive of any and all expenses that may arise. This list is a good start, however, and makes clear that the attorney's fees are not going to be applied to these costs. It is important that you instill this into the client's head before undertaking the representation.

Now that we are clear about expenses associated with the client's case, we need to consider how to arrange the payment of our fees. As research has shown, the traditional retainer for attorneys is dwindling.[1] Many attorneys are currently using alternative compensation arrangements (ACAs). Just an initial disclaimer: you should always consult with your jurisdiction's ethical opinions and/or bar rules for what types of fee agreements are permitted in your state.

WHAT ARE ALTERNATIVE COMPENSATION AGREEMENTS?

ACAs provide lawyers a system for compensation for the services provided. ACAs are arrangements between the attorney and client setting the guidelines of compensation using a structure other than the traditional system of

---

[1] Robert E. Hirshon, *The Billable Hour Is Dead. Long Live . . . ?* American Bar Association (Jan. 1 2013), www.americanbar.org/groups/gpsolo/publications/gp_solo/2013/january_february/billable_hour_dead_long_live/.

hourly billing. Even though the billable hour is used in the majority of law firms regardless of size, ACAs have existed for quite a while. The financial climate of the legal market, however, has made them increasingly popular once again.

The first thing we must remember is that ACAs are not about charging less than the hourly equivalent. It is an attempt to reach the middle ground that is acceptable to the client and the attorney at the moment of hiring the attorney. The ideal ACA should give realistic expectations for both the attorney and client not only on just costs, hours (not) billed, and work product, but, most importantly, on the value of the services. The perception of value, of course, is greatly subjective and, thus, the lawyer must invest time early on to calculate his/her ACA's value and sell this value to the client seeking his/her representation.

Further, the ACAs are not about exceeding more than what an hourly rate might be. This value should be founded on what is fair and reasonable both to the client and the lawyer. As the attorney, you should experiment with using your old billable hour cases. Maintaining an account of the billable time should be the lawyer's measure of cost, not necessarily a measure of the value they are providing the clients.

BENEFITS OF ACAs

The billable hour arrangement has exposed many challenges to both the client and the lawyer. When a client goes to a dentist or veterinarian or has a plumbing issue, they want to know "how much will this cost me?" All of these professions are capable of giving a definitive answer. Lawyers? Not so much. Our favorite response appears to be: "that depends." This response instills no confidence in the client to hire you to do the service. Furthermore, the incentive is for the lawyer to prolong the litigation and bill more hours to drain the retainer using possibly unnecessary tasks. The result is that the lawyer requests the retainer be replenished. This will cause the client/attorney relationship to deteriorate faster than other common reasons. Once you have engaged into an ACA, the incentive is on both ends to resolve the matter sooner than later. Clients typically do not wish to have their family law action continue needlessly for months and months when one possible hearing could resolve most of the contested issues in their case. The lawyer will want to resolve the case in the best-case scenario for the client in the least time as possible.

This is not to say there will not be outliers if you choose to engage in this billing structure. We will all get burned using this system at least once. You will complete a long case for peanuts sooner or later. The key is to determine the sweet spot of the price charged to ensure the attorney receives adequate compensation while providing the client with zealous advocacy and the attorney does not feel "burned out" or regretful.

One tip to help you find this sweet spot would be to review older cases and how much you typically billed for that particular case under similar circumstances. Did the case involve a contested child custody matter? Did the case involve a Guardian Ad Litem? Did the matter require expert testimony from a child psychologist that you prepared most of the night before trial to cross-examine? This will give you the road map to assess your price. Once you have the "ballpark" price of what you need for the matter, take a case for that price. Use it as the billing standard for future clients. If it goes well, do it again. If it does not work well, determine why it did not work. Make adjustments accordingly and you will find that sweet spot mentioned above. This method is great for transitioning from an hourly retainer to an ACA.

Another benefit you will notice when you convert to this billing structure: your client relations should improve. Money should cease to be an issue between you and the client. With a retainer up front in this structure, this also reduces and/or eliminates the chances of having to hound clients later for money owed. One of the biggest concerns family law attorneys have with the ACA billing structure is excessive communications. However, many clients in this case do not call about smaller issues like they do when you are billing per hour. This should be a welcome surprise! Of course, this may not be your experience. If you set the tone as suggested in chapter 1, however, you should be able to limit this issue.

EXAMPLES OF ACAs

ACAs come in different forms in practice. Here are some of the most common examples from family law.

Flat Fees

A flat fee is often used in transactional matters with a clearly defined service for a set price. You may choose to represent a client through an entire litigation of the matter start to finish for the set price. This is likely the easier flat fee to market your services for the client. They know they have an attorney no matter what happens in the case or how long the matter lasts.

Another model would be a "phased flat fee." This is where the attorney charges the client for stages of the litigation. You can set your fee for a period of time until a triggering event occurs. At that point, the client would need to pay for the next stage of the fee for the attorney's continued services or permit the attorney to withdraw from further representation. Attorneys will typically have a set price leading up to an initial temporary hearing. Completion of the hearing presents the perfect opportunity for the attorney and client to discuss whether or not the attorney will continue to represent the client and how much the next phase will cost. If you don't feel comfortable with the entire matter being handled for a set flat fee, this may be the ACA you need to test for flat fees. It gives you the opportunity to assess whether or not ACAs work for you and gives the perfect opportunity to withdraw from representation after the triggering event.

Subscription Fee Arrangement

Another flat-fee model is the subscription fee arrangement. This arrangement between the client and the attorney would be where the attorney agrees to essentially accept monthly fees that are set in advance for the client to subscribe to the attorney's time for his or her case. Think of it as the Netflix version of attorney's fees. This is for the client who may not be ready to hire an attorney full-time for their custody case but would like the advice and tips the attorney can assist with in the ongoing litigation. You can review any documents they have prepared, sell your form templates catered to their child custody matter, and provide coaching sessions for the subscriber.

Take caution against this model, however. You do not want to get pulled into the litigation by a judge for providing this ghost attorney service. Careful drafting on your engagement letter can limit your exposure if detailed enough. For further discussion of this type of billing of clients and limited representation, an excellent book, *Unbundled Legal Services: A Family Lawyer's Guide* by Forrest S. Mosten and Elizabeth Potter Scully, is available from the American Bar Association (ABA) Family Law Section as well. It is important to note that most states permit limited scope representation via their ethical rules. The ABA Model Rule 1.2(c) provides:

> ***(c) A lawyer may limit the scope of the representation if the limitation is reasonable under the circumstances and the client gives informed consent.***[2]

Many states have adopted this rule explicitly or a similar version. With this in mind, put exactly what you are doing for the client in writing and explain it to them. As long as it is in writing and is clear, this provides the attorney the ability to limit his or her scope and potential liability for the attorney.

RETAINERS

This model is the traditional one but merits discussion. This is the traditional bill by the hour to your client for your time spent on their matter. With technology cutting time down on tedious tasks (see chapter 3), this model may not be the best for your practice. Hourly rates don't allow your time to scale up your practice. It limits your time for other matters and opportunities. Charging an hourly rate arrangement means that your earnings will always be limited by the time you could possibly work on a matter.

With this form of billing, you should base your rate on your years and litigation experience, the market rate in your local area, the complexity of the custody case, and the temperament of the client upon meeting him/her.

Capped Hour Arrangement

A capped fee is very similar to the hourly rate. In this pricing model, a client will pay by the hour, but the number of hours the attorney will work is

---

[2] Center for Professional Responsibility, American Bar Association, Model Rules of Professional Conduct (2020).

capped at a preset limit. The client will pay either after the work is completed or when the capped hourly time is exhausted. The benefit to this structure is that clients will have peace of mind knowing they won't pay more than a certain amount per invoice. There are, however, some detriments to this model. It has all the detriments of charging by the hour in the traditional retainer arrangement; additionally, if a client expects to have a matter completed within the preset hours and the matter isn't, the relationship can take a downturn as trust is tested. Because the capped fee mark has passed, you are leaving yourself vulnerable to countless time-consuming communications that would otherwise have been tapered by the terms of the traditional fee agreement. Again, proceed with caution if you are a family law attorney considering using this billing structure.

Evergreen Retainer

An evergreen retainer is a type of security deposit for the attorney. Just like other types of retainers, your client pays you a lump sum at the initial hiring and the attorney uses this sum to pay his/her fees and expenses.

The difference is that with an evergreen retainer, the client needs to keep a predetermined minimum balance on the trust account to maintain the attorney–client relationship. The benefits of the Evergreen Retainer are:

- better collection rates for billable hours for the representation
- better client relationship than the traditional retainer model
- better cash flow for your law practice
- better flexibility for the client not having to pay large retainer sums,
- simplified trust accounting

This also keeps both the attorney's and the client's mind at ease as to whether there will be enough compensation to complete the necessary work in the case as it progresses. An example of an Evergreen Retainer clause you may wish to use:

> ***The Client agrees to an advance retainer deposit of $3,500 paid with the execution of this agreement and further agrees to replenish the retainer with a $1,500 payment when the retainer balance falls below $1,000. Failure to replenish shall stand as grounds for withdrawal of representation by the Attorney.***

Sliding Fee Scales Billable Hours

This type of relationship is where the attorney has ascertained the rough gross monthly income of the client. Make sure to get the client's income documentation at or before their initial consultation. For example, the person scheduling the consult should ask the client to provide the last three years of tax returns and their year-to-date pay statements. With these documents, the attorney then measures this income against the Federal Poverty Guidelines for that person's household size. From there, the attorney may come up with a percentage to charge the client based on this income. This may be a set price for the entire case as a "flat fee" or a monthly and/or hourly payment proportionate to his/her income. Once again, if you use this for the hourly arrangement, beware of the detriments of the traditional retainer noted above. This arrangement can be used for fulfilling the need of the modest-means client who too often goes *pro se* in family law litigation. Be sure to take the time and walk the client through the process on how you set the hourly fee should you choose to provide services that are billed hourly.

An example of the hourly rate sliding fee scale is displayed here:[3]

Family Household Size	125% FPL	150% FPL	175% FPL	200% FPL	250% FPL	300% FPL
1	$15,950	$19,140	$22,330	$25,520	$31,900	$38,280
2	$21,550	$25,860	$30,170	$34,480	$41,300	$51,720
3	$27,150	$32,580	$38,010	$43,440	$54,300	$65,160
4	$32,750	$39,300	$45,850	$52,440	$65,500	$78,600
5	$38,350	$46,020	$53,960	$61,360	$76,700	$92,040
6	$43,950	$52,740	$61,530	$70,320	$87,900	$105,480
Attorney Hourly Rate	*$90*	*$100*	*$125*	*$150*	*$175*	*$200*

Note: FPL = Federal Poverty Level

[3] https://aspe.hhs.gov/poverty-guidelines.

Combination of Flat Fee and Retainer

In this type of arrangement, the attorney will charge the client a set fee for some set services. If and when there is a triggering event, then a more traditional retainer arrangement takes over the attorney–client relationship. A common example of this arrangement would be a scenario where the attorney agrees to represent a client in a child custody matter that appears uncontested. Should the matter become contested at any point, the hourly billing method would take over the representation.

A word of caution here would be to make sure your engagement letter contains this language clearly so there is no confusion. A version of this language is as follows:

> *IT IS UNDERSTOOD that this contract is for limited scope representation (uncontested child custody modification) whereby the attorney's obligations to the client shall cease, and no refund shall be given in the event that the uncontested matter becomes contested on any substantive issue. "Contested" shall mean the matter requires mediation and/or litigation from attorneys, or any expenditure of time from attorneys above and beyond the terms of this contract.*
>
> *If any of the above events occur and/or are necessary, the client and attorney will consider the representation as a separate and new matter requiring a new fee agreement in which the attorney will bill the client at the rate of $250 per hour until final resolution of this matter. The attorney and client agree that both may terminate the representation should payment for contested services not occur as discussed.*

A detriment to this arrangement is that you have to now hound your child custody client for the new hourly fees when they may have spent their savings on the initial fee paid. Another detriment is the uncertainty of the cost now that you are charging per hour. A word of advice would be to sit the client down and discuss this arrangement upon the triggering event. Provide the signed engagement letter containing the clear language so your attorney–client relationship does not deteriorate. Most clients will appreciate the thoroughness before you begin billing them hourly. Should the triggering event occur, and the client be unwilling to pay an hourly rate, the triggering event could be the point where the representation may end amicably for the client and the attorney.

An easy example to give in these discussions would be the difference between negotiating the terms of a parenting or other such custody agreement with the other party and/or attorney, versus entering your appearance on a matter set in a contested custody track before the court. You can use the court events, like the due dates for a responsive pleading, or the date of a scheduling conference, as a triggering event. Be careful not to enter your court appearance or accept service on your client's behalf before this point, so that you are not at the mercy of the court to get out of the matter.

CONCLUSION

It is common to experiment with a few payment options, choosing the one that works best for you. Many lawyers have gone exclusively to a "flat-fee" system. This is not an easy choice, but for some it has proven successful. Traditional retainers are what most lawyers still use, but clients often find this billing system to be the most frustrating. They are shocked to see you actually billed that five-minute phone call for $25.00. Additionally, the flat-fee system gives you the opportunity to scale up your law practice. Gone are the days of recording all billable hours on cases for the week. You can now focus on what action is needed for your client. This permits you to accept additional clients that you may not have been able to accept under traditional retainers.

Of course, when switching to a flat-fee billing structure, you can still get burned on cases. You are committing yourself and your services to the client until the bitter end, which in the worst case can mean low/pro bono compensation. It will require the reviewing of many reports in your case management software before you come up with a successful flat fee that you find acceptable for representation for family law matters. Once this "sweet spot" is met, you will be able to relax on this part of the representation as the client will simply pay what you have settled on. The client enjoys the flat fee because they know exactly the cost of their particular case. With the money issue now gone for the client, that worry of calling the attorney and then being billed for it vanishes. You may find when you do this that the client does not call as much as you fear they will.

If you are fond of traditional retainers, the tips provided in this chapter can hopefully still allow you to maximize your legal skills for a client who is not as affluent as you may wish. Not only will your client be more satisfied that you were able to do more for them, you will be happier helping this person who cannot afford years-long litigation. Should you choose to try one of the ACAs above, please consult your local rules of professional conduct to ensure that the arrangement is permitted under your jurisdiction.

3

Must-Have Technology to Effectively Represent and Expedite (and Make Your Life Simpler)

Many state bar associations are now requiring attorneys to be competent in technology as part of their ethical obligations to their clients. Bottom line: do not shy away from technology, **EMBRACE IT!** Thankfully the days of typewriters and pagers are behind us in law practice. Our days are now filled with technology all around us. As legal practitioners, we can use this to our advantage to not only cut costs for our clients and reduce errors on our part, but also to give us back our sanity and reduce overall stress experienced by attorneys. This book is not meant to endorse any particular software mentioned. You are encouraged to try these and any others until you find the one that fits your style. Further, this chapter is not meant to be a testament of the authors' technology expertise. As many of you are learning on a daily basis, so are the authors.

This chapter will provide some key features of technology that could assist in the area of child custody litigation and your law practice overall.

CASE MANAGEMENT SOFTWARE

To maximize the delivery of big-budget results on a small retainer budget, the lawyer's office must be set up for success. This is where technology can be your friend. The days of slower communications by postal mail and awaiting replies from the other side are, fortunately, over. Aside from the obvious technology of email, there are now a variety of case management software applications available out there for your practice. If you currently do not use a version of case management software, try out a few to find one that suits your style and personality. Most offer a trial period when you can test out all the features to ensure the software is to your liking. The following list is not an exhaustive one, but rather to introduce you to the well-known ones on the market today:

- AbacusLaw
- Amicus Attorney
- CaseMap
- Clio
- Filevine
- MyCase
- PracticePanther
- Rocket Matter
- Smokeball
- Tabs3
- Zola Suite

Many of these softwares offer a "client portal" where the client can log in and see their case file instantly upon the attorney uploading them. Clients will appreciate being able to check on their case whenever they wish, and you will appreciate the client not calling daily asking if anything is happening. The portal can also provide convenient features for the client, including paying invoices for fees and expenses, sending secure messages to the attorney, and see upcoming events (meetings, depositions, court dates). The benefit for the client is most of these applications have an app for their cell phone to access their file at any time.

AUTOMATE DOCUMENT GENERATION

Another benefit for both the client and lawyer in a child custody case is the hours saved by creating the usual pleadings in a matter of seconds. Many of the case management applications listed here now include some version of a document assembly feature. The idea is that you can upload your standard "Petition for Modification of Custody," with the custom fields you create that allow you to simply generate the complete version by a few clicks of the mouse. From there, you can customize the various information to your client's unique situation. What used to cost the attorney an hour or two creating these documents has now been sliced to minutes. The client will be thankful for a smaller invoice and the attorney will be thankful for freed-up afternoons.

To further use technology in the child custody area to cut costs, use your discovery documents as your biggest tool in the war chest. Tailor your interrogatories and requests for production of documents to get *exactly* what is needed in your client's case. Many attorneys don't use this piece of advice enough and instead send out "blanket" discovery only to realize the one piece of evidence that would benefit their case wasn't covered in standard interrogatories/requests. If your opposing party is working late hours, request their work schedules from their employer, etc. This would be missed if you simply asked for their pay stubs. Proper use may reduce the need for more costly discovery including depositions.

HAVE YOUR CLIENT USE CO-PARENTING SOFTWARE

Another good way to have the client document all communication between the two parents is online co-parenting software. A few examples would be Our Family Wizard, coParenter, and Coparently, which both have an annual fee of approximately $100 a year. Talking Parents and App Close, which are free of charge, have fewer features than the paid version. While litigation is pending, these software tools can provide an outlet where the parents can communicate effectively and efficiently. The parents can schedule extracurricular activities for the children and track expenses such as summer camps. Some softwares even have the ability so one parent can pay the other for such expenses through the app. The software will maintain a record that can be easily printed for any subsequent hearings. These printouts are usually very easy for a judge to read. Further, the technology has added a Google Maps feature that will pinpoint the parent's physical location with date and time stamp to ensure that one parent actually showed up to an exchange and avoid the "he said/she said" argument in court concerning "no-shows."

Should the case be highly contentious, it may be advisable to the client to keep the software post-litigation for any future contempt and/or modifications. The application Our Family Wizard provides a unique feature called the ToneMeter™, which highlights any emotionally charged language while drafting messages to the other parent. It functions like a spell check for contentious language. It is an ideal recommendation at the close of high-conflict cases for the parties to improve their communication moving forward. coParenter also offers a unique option for an on-demand virtual mediator to help resolve disputes. Both of these features minimize the need for the parties to turn to their respective counsel over every minor conflict post-judgment.

TEXT MESSAGE/PHONE CALL LOG BACKUP SOFTWARE

Text messages, phone logs, and photographs taken on phones have become increasingly prominent in discovery requests and for use as evidence at trial. There are several types of backup software that allow you to view and extract information backed up on your phone: for example, iBackup Viewer, Droid Transfer, and SMS Backup+. This is helpful to have, or have your client download, for retrieval of entire text message threads between the parties and others. There are a number of reasons why obtaining text messages in this manner is favorable. First, it saves your client hours of screenshotting texts between them and the opposing party, and thereby, saving them on the fees for you to upload, organize, and review each individual screenshot. Second, many times you can get the specific times, dates, and the phone numbers for each individual message sent, which is not always provided in the screenshots, especially with an iPhone log.

It is helpful to use backup software to get the whole call logs between the parties when proof is needed that attempts to contact the other parent were made. If your client relies only on the call logs on their phones, that information will get removed over time. Using photographs extracted by the backup software will also get you the metadata for each photograph so you can prove the time, place, and location where certain photographs were taken. This is particularly helpful for photographs taken of injuries in domestic violence disputes.

CLOUD STORAGE

Rather than having multiple filing cabinets in your office, you may want to consider opting for an effective digital collection stored on a cloud storage platform. Depending on the storage space needed for your firm, you could use this software for no cost, as many storage companies provide a certain amount of no-cost storage. Should your firm outgrow this space, you can upgrade your free account to a paid version for a very low price. The cost savings of cloud storage is high. It leads to a reduction in information technology costs because you no longer have to pay to set up, maintain, or back up your personal servers, and it provides the ability to avoid purchasing costly hardware that will quickly become obsolete.

Cloud storage also provides better accessibility for a firm, because you can work from any location where you have access to the internet. Another feature allows both clients and attorneys the ability to easily share files that cannot be emailed because they are too large or contain confidential information. Cloud storage also provides greater disaster recovery in the event of a computer failure or other natural disasters. Should any of these happen, your practice can be up and running on a new computer as quickly as you can provide internet access to it.

Lastly, a cloud storage service provides necessary security to protect confidential information for your practice. Reputable online data storage companies are able to provide robust physical security measures than a solo practitioner or small firm can afford. Many reputable online data storage companies use cutting-edge security technologies, such as two-factor authentication for logging in and encryption of files stored on the server.

ELECTRONIC SIGNING SOFTWARE

Gone are the days of requiring your client to come by the office to sign one document needed for their case. Should your jurisdiction permit electronic signing for documents, this can cut down time for case management.

You can simply send the relevant documents to your clients and have them sign them at their convenience online. Some examples include AdobeSign, DocuSign, HelloSign, E-Sign Genie, and SignEasy.

With these tools, you simply upload the document that needs the client's signature, set the spots that the client needs to initial and sign, and email it to the client via the software. The client receives an email containing a link to the document. The client then "adopts" an electronic signature to use for the signing and/or draws their own e-signature for usage. After a few clicks on the designated signature lines, the client has completed the signing process from the convenience of their phone or laptop. This software is great for getting the engagement letter signed on the spot.

Clients who have a Gmail address can also download the DocHub extension, which allows the client to sign electronically onto PDF files sent to them and save the document to their Google Drive.

ONLINE CALENDARING/BOOKING SOFTWARE

Making the process of setting up an initial consultation for a potential client easy makes a great first impression. One way of doing this is to set up an online booking feature clients can use twenty-four hours a day/seven days per week. Some examples of this type of software are: Accuity, PickTime, SetMore, LawTap, and BookMe, just to name a few. These calendar booking tools use your Google Calendar, Outlook calendar, etc. to maintain up-to-date availability for the attorney without the need to call your office and have your assistant set the appointment for you. Having a feature on the menu tab of your website as "Book an Appointment" gives the prospective client the ability to set the appointment for a day and time that works best for their own schedule. Another feature of some of these softwares is it allows for consultation payment for new clients.

For current clients, you have the ability to place a link in your signature block of emails for clients to click and set up a meeting with you for a future date. This ends the seemingly endless "Does Tuesday at __ p.m. work for you?" emails. Most of the online booking software contains the added feature of "reminder" emails for the client. This will ensure the least amount of no-shows as possible for your practice.

CREDIT CARD PROCESSING

If you are only permitting your client to pay you via cash and check, you're missing out on a major sector of potential clients. Credit card processing for law firms has never been easier. Some companies are now marketing their software to law firms as they have the capability of sending the incoming money to your operating account or trust account at your discretion. Taking payments via credit card gives the client the ability to pay the full retainer fee and still break down the payments into smaller monthly increments.

Much like the online booking software, the credit card processing software lets you place a "Make a Payment" tab on your website menu for clients to pay you directly through your credit card processing company. You can also add the payment feature into the signature block of the emails you send to prospective and current clients, making the entire process easier for them.

ONLINE INTAKE FORMS

Another feature you may wish to consider is online intake forms. These forms can expedite the acquisition process for your practice. The forms gather all of the initial names, addresses, phone numbers, dates of birth, etc. that you would need should the client actually hire you at the initial consult, thus saving valuable time. You may choose to create your intake forms through paid software. Should you wish to employ a free version, you may wish to consider Google Forms, contained within the G-Suite collection of apps. From there, you simply email the online intake form to the prospective client. Tailor the intake specifically for items of child custody that would arise. See the Appendix for an example. Consider creating an intake form for each practice area of your firm to send to the applicable prospective client.

CUSTOMER RELATIONSHIP MANAGEMENT SOFTWARE

Given the need for online intake, a software may be useful for your practice. Customer relationship management (CRM) software is a tool for managing all your firm's relationships and interactions with current and potential clients. Not every new potential client signs up with your firm right away. After an initial call or consult, they may be hesitant to sign with your firm. This is a place where many firms tend to drop the ball. They put the burden of follow-up on the client and fail to follow up. Remembering to follow up with potential clients can be a bit time consuming, but it will result in more retained clients. A CRM software application helps you with the follow-up process and moves your clients through the "pipeline" using automated features. With workflow automation, you can automatically send potential clients personalized-yet-automated emails once they get to a certain stage in the intake process to help them complete their intake journey. As an example, once a client schedules an initial consult, you can send them a new consult template with accompanying appointments, tasks for you to complete, and automated emails and documents sent out to the client. This feature also reduces the chances that you are subject to one of the top complaints about family law attorneys, the failure to communicate effectively with the client.

The goal is to improve business relationships. A CRM system can help your firm stay connected to clients, streamline the onboarding processes, and improve profitability for the firm while cutting costs for the client. Typical features of a CRM designed for law firms include:

- Client Intake Forms to email the prospective client
- management of all your contacts from "new potential client" to "engaged client"
- tracking where your clients learn about your firm to ensure that your marketing efforts are providing you a return on your investment
- follow-up emails to prospective clients for further engagement
- integration with case management software mentioned in this section to ensure a seamless process of prospective client intake to the moment they become a current client
- email campaigns that can keep you fresh in the mind of your clients for potential referrals in the future
- online booking

PARENTING TIME SOFTWARE

As most states require a visitation schedule/parenting plan as part of any final resolution for a child custody case, a detailed plan is necessary to ensure one parent doesn't lose valuable parenting time with the child(ren).

You can design your own parenting schedule template for use in child custody cases or you may wish to employ the use of technology to ensure no detail goes unnoticed. Examples of this kind of software include Custody X Change and Kids First! This software provides advanced calculations for parenting time between the parties through court-ready plans and reports. The software also provides the client, opposing party, and the court a clear breakdown using visual aspects including colors to designate each parent's time with the child(ren). Once this schedule is adopted by the court or consented to by the parents, it may be uploaded onto the software's app which provides it to the client on their mobile device.

In addition to the specific calendar of parenting time between the parties, this software provides state-specific boilerplate language requirements for the plan. These software products also have built-in language for a wide variety of situations that the practitioner may forget to include. Such situations include international travel, passport requirements, long-distance co-parenting configurations, and notification requirements for parents for extracurricular activities/education issues just to name a few. This software can ensure that none of these provisions fall silent in your draft parenting time schedule, to avoid disputes in the future.

FINANCIAL DISCLOSURE AFFIDAVIT AUTOMATION

As you are probably aware, financial disclosures are required of both parents in a child custody litigation to calculate the appropriate amount of child support. When starting out practicing child custody, some lawyers will require the client to take a blank affidavit home and have the client fill it out to the best of their ability. You will quickly learn that this is not very effective. Affidavits are received with scribbled writing all over, inaccurate math calculations for expenses, and illegible writing. Of course, there is a better solution for this requirement. This is where technology can save you so much time. Should you also provide services in other areas of family law including divorce, you may wish to acquire software to manage the finances of the marital estate. Some examples include: Family Law Software, PartUs, and EasySoft. These provide the ability to email the client a link. When the client clicks the link, the software (via the cloud) will guide them through their income and expenses sections. As long as the client is inputting the correct amounts into the expenses, the calculations will be correct. After the client completes the affidavit online, you receive an emailed notification for you to download the completed affidavit to print for trial and settlement negotiations. The sheer amount of time you will save using one of these software tools will be invaluable. Using them for divorce is wise, but they work just as effectively for child custody litigation. The affordability is also a selling point, as many of these programs cost less than $100 per month at the time of writing.

Workflow Tracker and Deadline Trackers

If you are like many lawyers and wake up in the middle of the night convinced you forgot to do something this week, you desperately need to set up a checklist/workflow system within your practice. If you decide to acquire a case management software application, make sure this is a feature it contains. If you spend a few hours at the beginning and set up checklists for each type of matter you handle, you can rest better at night knowing every task is completed as required. Further, if you know you have trial deadlines, set the counter that can auto-remind you to ensure no deadline goes missed.

LOOK OUT FOR COMMON SOFTWARE HACKS

So many law firms function off Microsoft Office; but whatever software your office uses, make sure you (and your staff) are familiar with what hacks can make billable tasks far quicker. For example, Outlook allows for letter templates. Even though you should carefully explain the significance of each legal document to a client with particularity to their own case, there are common themes. You can create templates for an explanation of each document, so, for example, if you get the other side's answer to your custody complaint, you should have general text explaining the function of their answer and what it means for the rest of the legal proceedings. A PDF-to-Word converter is endlessly helpful in preparing your own discovery responses. If there are phrases you find yourself needing to type in again and again, consider creating keyboard shortcuts or keeping Microsoft Sticky Notes with the phrases on there to cut and paste into your document. If you, or your staff, are well versed in the many efficient ways technology can speed up the process on your end, it will help expedite your case overall.

COURT-MANDATED REMOTE HEARINGS

Court closures due to COVID-19 have forced nearly every jurisdiction to implement some type of remote way to handle uncontested hearings and some even for evidentiary hearings. For scheduling conferences, the use of remote hearings and requiring counsel only attendance have saved litigants not only money on fees, but also the emotional toll of having to be in the same room as their ex. Despite scheduling conferences consisting of picking dates, there is still contention in the air once both parties are in the same room. Countless clients tell their lawyers they feel like they "lost" at scheduling conferences, simply because the other party or their attorney was speaking out of turn. The use of remote hearings saves the client on your fees for travel time as well as for the time spent waiting in court for your case to be called. If remote uncontested hearings remain an option in your jurisdiction, you can always try to stipulate with opposing counsel and make a request that the court hear the matter remotely.

Just a reminder for busy practitioners: **KEEP YOUR OFFICE CLEAN!** There is nothing more unappealing than to look professional in a suit and have the office (real or at home) untidy or have files stacked up in the background. Consider a virtual background, available in many of the videoconferencing software applications, that makes your background much more professional in the event you cannot clean up. Also safeguard against any potential interference. Let everyone else in the office know you are not to be disturbed while on your call. Print out a "Do Not Disturb" or "Court in Session" sign and tape it outside of your closed door. This is further discussed in chapter 11.

MENTAL HEALTH APPS FOR YOU AND YOUR CLIENT

With all of the foregoing discussion of technology, it must be mentioned that sometimes you need to disconnect for a moment and recharge. For this, you can try out a few mental health/meditation apps, if you feel it would help.

These apps are very affordable (most under $20 per month). They can guide you in that 10- to 15-minute recharge that many lawyers need when the stress and anxiety of law practice presents itself throughout the day. Please explore the research on all the benefits of meditation for reduction of stress, depression, and anxiety. We could all use decreases in depression, stress, and anxiety in our lives, and these apps can greatly help with that goal. Be sure to recommend them to your stressed client as well. If they are calm, they are less likely to call you out of stress with the custody case.

CONCLUSION

The authors do not claim to be technology experts by any means. The technology suggested in this chapter can, however, make your life and practice much easier. The technology listed also can lead to a better impression for your client. The biggest tip from this is to try out the different software and find the one that fits you best. Lastly, try to view any technology acquired for your practice as an investment rather than another overhead cost.

4

Use No- and/or Low-Cost Methods for Factual Development

There are more sources for factual development beyond witness testimony, financial disclosure affidavits, banking statements, and other items readily accessible to the client. It is advantageous for the attorney to compile evidence that will help the client's case. The one benefit to this area of law is that courts have a very low bar on admissible evidence. This chapter is here to give you some creative ideas on how best to build a child custody argument for trial. Some ideas may even seem far-fetched. The goal should remain that we, as child custody litigators, leave no stone unturned. Our clients only know what they know. We should complete the initial intake of them and then begin our in-depth research to develop the structure of our argument.

The following examples of evidence may serve your case well and are available at low to no cost for the attorney and client. Consider the tips to stack up the evidence in your favor.

PUBLIC RECORDS

In family disputes where at least one party is of modest means—or the case is a high-conflict one—there is a substantial likelihood that the family has at some point enlisted the assistance of a public agency or government entity at least once. Although not a happy circumstance for the parties, this does come with several advantages for the cost-conscious attorney. Chief among these are the records that are typically generated by those entities. These records can be some of the most valuable evidence available in a custody dispute, for several reasons:

Factual records already exist.

Police departments, community services agencies, housing authorities, etc. must keep records of their activities. To the extent that they provide or administer benefits or are charged with public safety, these agencies have due process obligations toward those who benefit from their services. The records they keep, therefore, *should* be specific and detailed. The attorney can then rely on these for a great deal of information rather than spending time interviewing witnesses, obtaining subpoenas, or drafting affidavits. The report will provide the insight you need to determine whether or not to subpoena individual witnesses to testify in person or via affidavit at a hearing. The reports can also alert you to whether your client may have had the inaccurate version of any incident.

Accessible and low cost.

Agencies might charge a nominal fee (e.g., per page) for physical copies of records, but they should not otherwise request any other costs for the preparation of public records. You can also send your client to obtain the documents to avoid billing attorney time (they may also be free for the client to obtain). Last, but certainly not least, obtaining these records can help you avoid time-consuming and costly discovery disputes.

Admissible as hearsay exceptions.

Depending on your state's rules of evidence, records that constitute first-hand knowledge or observations of a public official while exercising the duties of their office are likely to be exceptions to the hearsay rule. A certified copy from the custodian of the records will often be admissible on its face. Of course, watch out for double hearsay!

Observations are considered highly credible.

The firsthand observations of law enforcement and other public employees made pursuant to duty have a de facto presumption of reliability in the eyes of most judges. Subpoena the actual official should it serve your case well. It could make the difference in your case.

Some examples of these records that you may wish to consider include:

911 reports and call transcripts or recordings

- Police Computer-Aided Dispatch Reports
- Incident reports from police
- Incident reports from school law enforcement
- Incident reports from apartment complex or neighborhood security
- BODYCAM footage from any officer and/or security camera footage
- Arrest warrants
- Records from housing authorities and other community support agencies
- Educational records

OTHER PUBLIC RESOURCES

With a few precautions, public entities can provide additional support for both the case and the family. For example, when serving a complaint, always make attempts at service through the applicable law enforcement agency before engaging a private process server. You can also usually convince law enforcement to make multiple attempts, especially if you ask nicely or have additional information relevant to service.

Faith organizations can provide additional support, if appropriate for the family in question. If clients are amenable to seeing a counselor but cannot afford a professional, a faith leader may be able to step in. These organizations can also assist with visitation exchanges or perhaps supervised visitation. Of course, use your judgment, and encourage clients to use theirs.

PRIOR ORDERS REGARDING THE SAME PARTIES

If your action involves a modification of custody from a prior court order, you will obviously need the prior order. Don't stop there; get the entire docket file from the prior action. If applicable, call the original attorney (if you weren't that attorney) and find out their thoughts on the prior action. The former attorney can provide insight to your client that you may not be aware of after the initial meeting. Get as much information as you possibly can about the prior case. If you are able and the client can afford it, it may be beneficial to acquire the prior case court transcript. You will get a read of your own client's ability to testify as well as the other parent's skill. Apply this information to all cases including any temporary protective orders, multiple court actions, or child support actions. You will get a better timeline of the two parties' interactions as well as learn information you may not have got otherwise. Prior child support actions can show whether or not the parents have possibly suppressed income over time.

DEPARTMENT OF LABOR STATISTICS ON SALARIES FOR CHILD SUPPORT

Another free resource to use for imputing wages against an obligor of child support is to use the United States Bureau of Labor Statistics for assistance with average salaries.[1] These statistics can be narrowed by geographical region and actual job title. Check your individual state evidence laws, but many states now allow this data as a reliable resource for employment income for an obligor.

LAND RECORDS

If you are lucky enough to live in a jurisdiction that has statewide publicly available land records online, for no cost to download, congratulations! These records are highly useful in custody and divorce cases alike. First, if you are having trouble locating another party, the land records may help. But also, for child support purposes, if one party is claiming to be impoverished, the land records will show what kind of property they are able to afford. Looking up the land on real estate websites will show you what it costs to reside there and gives you an idea if they may be living beyond what they may just be purporting to have. The same can be said for motor vehicle

[1] https://www.bls.gov/.

records if your client is complaining about the other parent's new luxury ride. Finally, if there is a judgment awarded against the other party, land records will be helpful for finding out what properties your client will be able to get a lien against.

CLIENT JOURNAL

One of the first homework assignments that can be given to a client leaving the office is for them to maintain a journal. These journals can be the traditional ones sold in stores. They can also be used electronically. The idea when having a client maintain entries is to develop the timeline as the case progresses. This piece of evidence can be used in most jurisdictions under the Rules of Evidence as a Writing Used to Refresh a Witness's Recollection (Federal Rules of Evidence Rule 612). Further, read the journals for potential witnesses the client may not even realize they should use. Make sure they include the exact dates and keep their entries in chronological order. Typical items to include in the client document are:

- Drop-off/Pick-up of the child. Include the time and if the other party stated anything noteworthy.
- Daily caretaking of the minor child. Have the client document their daily activities with the minor child. This will include who cooked for the child, who bathed the child, who took the child to school, who took them to the doctor appointment, and who put the child to bed.
- Telephone communication attempts and duration of the call. If the call does not take place, have the client note the attempts.
- Demeanor and visual cues. Should the call/video conference take place with the child, have the client note demeanor and any visual cues the parent may notice via the video.
- Extracurricular activities. Note what time the game/event was, who came to the event, what time the other party arrived, any guests with the other parent, and what time everyone departed. If there was a confrontation, write all details down.
- Appearance of the child. Pictures may not always be available. Have the client write down details of any rashes, cuts, bruises, and any other markings on the child's body. Also keep any notes of how the child was in appearance including torn and/or dirty clothing. Also

note if the child is unclean or unkempt. Tell the client to follow up their impression with the other parent/party to maintain simultaneous documentation of the event.

- Any items/clothing not returned from the parenting time with the other party. If you keep a detailed inventory of the items that went with the child to the other parent's house, you will know what did not return with the child. Write this incident down. Your client will sound much more educated in the courtroom if they can give dates, items, etc. of these kinds of incidents.
- Calendars. The client can use an empty calendar and color code the schedules that each party exercised and can include specific notes for certain incidents or missed visits.

Cost-Saving Tip: **You may wish to purchase a box of cheap composition notebooks to provide to the client. Buying in bulk will make the individual price lower. Many online stores like Amazon have bulk purchasing available for these notebooks. Providing a "free" one to your client gives no reason why your client cannot keep a journal out of laziness of buying one and/or price concerns. At the time of writing, you can purchase a 12-pack online for less than $30.00 plus shipping and handling.**

EDUCATION RECORDS

If the minor child is of school age, subpoena the educational records of the child's school. There are times when a client is sure to lose their case but may have their chances revived upon the introduction of the school records. Many report cards, progress reports, etc., include the daily attendance record for the child. Have your client check their calendar to see who had the child for the missed days. If the absences are during the other parent's access, this will add a powerful punch to your client's case for custody.

Look at every document in the package. Pay close attention to who is on the registration list, the emergency contacts, and any other list of individuals who are authorized to pick up and drop off. Oftentimes, if the parents were split up when the kids were enrolled in school, you will notice that the parent doing the enrolling will leave the other parent out altogether. In one case, the father enrolled the child in school in his school district without having the legal custody to do so. In the child's enrollment paperwork, he filled it out without acknowledging the mother on any level. The child's name excluded her middle name that was the same as her mother's. He did list her mother's name on the form but put his contact information as hers to appear as if they lived together. He even went so far as to only include his race and not check off the mother's. It was pointed out each time he ignored the mother in cross examination. It is easy to use these kinds of documents to allude to parental alienation without having the psychological experts to outright say it.

Send the client to the child's school to retrieve the records early. Should the records not serve any point at trial, you have lost nothing. If they are critical of the other side, send an official subpoena to get the Custodian of the Records Certificate to authenticate the documents to avoid the hearsay rule in most jurisdictions. From there, structure your cross-examination of the other party to walk through absences and any classes the child may be falling behind in to make your client's case.

SCHOOL RATINGS

While you are researching education records of the child, you may also wish to consider researching the actual school. Should the child go to a failing institution, bring this information out if it helps your client. This would be especially true if the child would relocate to a better school if placed with your client. This evidence can be used both ways in trial.

Should the child be homeschooled by a parent, do your research on the actual company who designed the curriculum. Most of the companies that produce the curriculum can produce information by request. Ensure the company is recognized by your state to ensure the child is not being scammed by a fly-by-night organization.

Get your client to do some internet research. You may be able to get their research into testimony regarding the rankings of the schools. If their school is higher ranked than the school in the other parent's area, it is worth it to bring up in their direct examination.

CHILDCARE FACILITIES

Upon learning of any childcare facility from your client, do your own research on the actual facility. Complete an internet search for the facility under the "news" tab. You may be shocked to learn information even the parents weren't aware of.

You should also do a docket search in the jurisdiction where the facility is located. Many facilities are routinely sued for the acts of an employee and/or administrators. Find out all you can to add to your arsenal of information regarding the matter.

Just like school records, enrollment records are important. Look and see if the parent enrolling the child even included the other as an authorized person to pick up the child. Whose address is used? Is the other parent listed as an emergency contact? Is the other parent even listed as the other parent, or is that space left blank? Carefully examine each document because you don't want to miss out on potential microaggressions by the registering parent.

RELIGIOUS INSTITUTIONS

The information above concerning childcare facilities should be reiterated here for religious institutions that the parent may expose the child to. Ensure the institution has not had their own legal controversy recently.

Further research to ensure the religious institution does not engage in any activities that the child should not be exposed to (e.g., snake handling, gay conversion therapy, etc.). Should you find any shocking information, use this against the perpetrating parent on cross-examination at any hearing or deposition. It should go without saying but consider the judge in your case. If the court is in a more rural area with a more conservative judge, this may not be the path you wish to take in your advocacy. If the judge is more progressive, consider exposing this information for a special clause in any parenting time plan of the court to not allow the minor child to be exposed to this activity. One way of completing this would be to permit your client to have the religion tie-breaking authority under legal custody to ensure no violation of the other parent's constitutional rights.

CRIME RATES AND OTHER INFORMATION FOR THE AREA OF A PARENT'S RESIDENCE

You will likely know the physical address of the other party from your client. Don't stop there. Actually research the address and see if there may be some undiscovered gold mine in a public search for critical information. Look online for crime maps for the geographical area. Most city and county areas have crime statistics. Some have even "mapped" the actual criminal incidents. Use this to your advantage if the opposing party lives in a relatively higher crime area of the town. You may also attempt to introduce this evidence in the inverse if your client's residence is a relatively peaceful area. This information is especially useful in a relocation custody matter where your client cannot investigate for themselves due to distance.

As with the crime statistics, you also should consider researching the other party's residence in relation to the state's sex offender registry. You may reveal that the other party lives next door to someone convicted of child molestation. Of course, the judge can consider some safety protocols should that parent wish to remain at that residence, given the newly learned information about the neighbors. This information can also be used to compare and contrast the numbers of offenders in one parent's area versus the number in the other parent.

CERTIFIED CRIMINAL CONVICTIONS

As President Ronald Reagan famously said, "Trust but verify." We should trust our clients but verify everything they say to us. Ask your client if the other parent has any criminal history. You will get an answer which they think is correct. Verify the answer against what public records show, however. The client may think their ex had a shoplifting charge a "few years ago." They may be shocked to learn that the parent was charged with shoplifting AND possession of narcotics. Once you find records within a courthouse, have the client go and get them in its entirety (as stated in chapter 1, send your client as the runner to save the attorney's time). Make sure they get a certified copy of the conviction, as it usually permits the documents to become admissible without objection. Should the matter not have a conviction, do not let this stop you from investigating it further. Most states permit asking a witness about an arrest even if no conviction occurred, because the evidence bar is usually very low as it relates to the best interest of the child standard.

DOCKET SEARCH FOR THE OPPOSING PARTY'S NEW SIGNIFICANT OTHER

Oftentimes, a child custody litigation manifests after a parent begins dating someone new. One parent will not want their child to be around "that man/woman." It is crucial that we, as lawyers, investigate the new character in the case. One way of doing this is to investigate public records in the courthouse of the county of the new individual. You may learn that this person was convicted of domestic violence two years ago for their ex and their children. Many courts now have online records dating back years. Don't just search the one county where the case sits. You can search within the surrounding county area to ensure you're not missing information. Don't settle for just criminal records. If the person is divorced as well, the divorce pleadings can provide insight for this matter. The person's ex may be your new best friend and witness for your client.

This information can be useful for your child custody case for not only the new significant other, but also any roommates, close friends, babysitters/childcare facility workers, and family members who reside with the parent. Essentially, anyone who will be exposed to the child(ren) should be closely looked at and made part of the case.

SOCIAL MEDIA OF ALL PARTIES

Before officially requesting social media profiles through the process of discovery, you should do your own "discovery." Look up all parties (including your own client) in the obvious social media outlets. Don't just stop at your client and the other parent, research significant others, babysitters of the child, and anyone living in the same household as the parties. Should the person not have their privacy settings set to a strict status, you may be able to view their entire profile without "adding" them as a friend on social media. Do not forget the professional social media (e.g., LinkedIn) as well. The parent may have their entire resume listed in the event they have voluntarily suppressed their income to minimize child support in the custody case.

Further, should the parent have a "public" social media with damning posts, print them now. Once they are served with a spoliation letter and/or formal discovery, they may attempt to "clean up" their page. Your printing of the earlier posts will serve you well on cross-examination at any hearing and/or deposition.

Lastly, do an actual internet search and find out if the opposing party has an online blog. This is a usually unchecked goldmine as well. It is quite shocking how much people will document their entire life into an online public journal. Many lawyers have experience finding this evidence searching online for that parent. Print all instances of the parent degrading your client, frustrations with the court process, evidence of intentional withholding the child from visitation, and evidence of drug/alcohol usage by the parent. This kind of documented evidence has turned around more than a few cases from potentially losing at trial.

PHYSICAL/MENTAL HEALTH OF THE OTHER PARENT

Typically, your client knows what ailments the other parent suffers from. These may be physical and/or mental ailments. Once your client provides this information, educate yourself.

Should the parent suffer from a mental health issue, you may wish to consult with the Diagnostic and Statistical Manual of Mental Disorders (DSM-5) from the American Psychiatric Association to learn all you can about the disorder they suffer from. Learn all limitations that the disorder may cause. Learn any and all treatments available to the disorder, including prescribed medications. Learn the side effects of any medication prescribed. You don't need the opposing side to be a medical doctor to have them thoroughly cross-examined about their knowledge of the disorder and whether or not they are following a treatment regimen. Not only will you sound better on cross-examination for this particular issue, you will be educating the judge in the case. As long as you can tie the parent's mental health disorder to their effectiveness as a parent, it should be admissible.

The same process should be applied to physical issues and/or physical disabilities to which the other parent may be diagnosed. Tie it directly to their ability to parent. Again, the more educated you are in a topic, the better your cross-examination will become in trial.

NEEDS OF THE MINOR CHILD

The tips concerning physical and mental health of the parent should be followed for any special needs and/or diagnoses for the minor child in the matter. Don't just stop at physical and mental health here. Explore the needs in relation to dietary restrictions and any special treatment necessary for his/her education. Doing your homework now will allow you to quiz the other parent in the case about the needs of the minor child. It also permits you to get your client educated about any condition to sound better in their testimony. If there are any specialists the child is in regular contact with, make sure your client knows who they are, and they know your client. If the child has an individualized education program (IEP), make sure your client is in every meeting and knows each member of the team. Typically, the records for these meetings will reflect who was there.

OTHER PARENT'S INSTABILITY OF HOUSING

Should your office invest funds into a legal research engine that contains some sort of person locator, use this feature until your fingers fall off. This feature typically lists all known addresses of a person and includes dates of residence. Should the parent have six homes within a year, use this evidence on cross-examination to your advantage. Your client may have been blind to the other parent moving around so much. This feature is not only available on expensive legal research search engines. You may also wish to perform a quick internet search for an address locator of a person. The only unfortunate part of this would be the cheaper/free options may not be as thorough. Consider weighing the cost of a better search engine against the benefits that come from having the software.

EVIDENCE OF AVAILABLE EXTRACURRICULAR ACTIVITIES

Should you represent a client in a relocation case seeking custody, you may wish to find out what available extracurricular options there may be in the client's new town (or lack thereof of the other parent's residence). A quick internet search for activities the child is interested in can provide schedules of any camps, activities, etc. Be sure to include in your research any costs, requirements, age limits, etc. of the activity for the minor child. Share the research with the client and make sure they are informed and able to articulate the information to share with the court at the hearing. This information will show the client to be a very informed parent and interested in having the child thrive.

DEPARTMENT OF FAMILY AND CHILDREN SERVICES RECORDS

Your client may or may not know of the other parent's involvement with the Department of Family & Children Services. One typical recommendation would be to issue a quick subpoena to the Department early in the case for any and all records containing the other parent's name. A lot of times, you may not get any results. Other times, you get a gold mine your client did not know about. The records should contain all contacts the Department made with the other parent, the circumstances of the investigation, and any potential witnesses unknown to your client. Attached in the Appendix is a sample subpoena for your use to tailor to your jurisdiction.

It should be noted, however, that the attorney for the Department will likely file an objection with the court in your case. Most federal and state statutes prohibit disclosure of social services records. However, a court can order, when, where, how, and to whom they are disclosed. Always file a responsive pleading to this objection asking that the court permit the records to be admitted under seal of the court. In the alternative, at least ask that the documents be disclosed to the judge and attorneys only without disclosure or dissemination. This will likely get the records in to your client's benefit. The benefits of the court's knowledge of all pertinent facts will substantially outweigh any risks by having the documents sealed.

INTERNATIONAL RELOCATION MATTERS

If relocation matters weren't tough enough for a court to decide, a parent moving over international borders makes it even tougher. The court in your jurisdiction probably does not know much about the new country in which the child may be relocated. This is where you, as the attorney, can educate the court. A suggested starting place may be the United States Department of State website for any travel advisories for the new country.[2] This website maintains up-to-date information about any risks of traveling to the country.

Further, verify the new country at issue has joined the Hague Abduction Convention to ensure a safe return of the minor child in the event the child visits with the parent in that country.[3] This information will weigh heavy on the court's mind should the country not ensure this protection.

These are the first pieces of information you should consider in an international relocated custody matter. Once you have this information, continue the research into crime statistics, any religious laws the country may have, education in the country, etc. By the time the trial should occur, you should have become an expert in the new country.

CONCLUSION

The resources in this chapter will, we hope, serve you well in your attempt to build a winning custody case without spending much, if any, funds from your client. You will appear much more informed about your client's matter and have ammunition against the other party that the client did not have knowledge of before hiring you. Take these tips and be creative in your research!

---

[2] https://travel.state.gov/content/travel/en/traveladvisories/traveladvisories.html/.

[3] U.S. Dep't of State, Understanding the Hague Convention, https://travel.state.gov/content/travel/en/Intercountry-Adoption/Adoption-Process/understanding-the-hague-convention/convention-countries.html.

5

Discovery and How to Effectively Get Your Needed Evidence

The scariest part of a custody trial is that it's your client's word against the other parent's. No one outside of those living in the home can truly know what happens behind closed doors. Both the credibility of your client and sufficient evidence are invaluable here. Your case can live or die in the discovery process alone. Knowing and utilizing the discovery tools that will get you the information you need are indispensable in a custody case and may also give you the leverage you need to settle your case.

TOOLS OF DISCOVERY

Depending on what your jurisdiction will allow, knowing the types of discovery you can propound is where you need to begin your case. The tools of discovery vary from jurisdiction to jurisdiction, but there are definitely predominantly popular tools throughout. There are tools for written discovery, meaning you will just have to respond to questions from the other side under oath. The main tools for written discovery are Interrogatories and

Requests for Admission of Facts. The other tools include Requests for Production of Documents, which are literally just that—documents you need to provide, and depositions, which are discussed in detail in the next chapter. There is also the use of subpoenas, which you can send to third parties to get documents that are relevant to your case without having to engage in a long drawn-out discovery battle.

Interrogatories

Interrogatories are questions answered under oath. Typically, your local rules will impose a limit of roughly 25 to 30 interrogatories that you may propound.[1] In some jurisdictions, there are forms for Domestic Relations Interrogatories available.[2] These are both helpful and hurtful. They are helpful in that you can save your clients money by using the forms. Acknowledging that these are standard form interrogatories will also show the opposing counsel that barring exceptional circumstances, there is little chance that any objection they make will be upheld.

These forms can be hurtful as well. In Maryland, the form interrogatories are primarily applicable to divorce. Questions that address issues like alimony and division of assets are not applicable. Frequently, and incorrectly, interrogatories will refer to your client as the "spouse." A response of "Not applicable" is appropriate here if your client and the opposing party are not at that time (or have never been) married. Time after time, opposing counsel propounds these form interrogatories with the service of their initial pleadings to ensure that they are received. The problem with this practice is that it ignores the intricacies and facts of your specific case. While the assurance that their interrogatories were received in service may be beneficial to the other side, they are ignoring the opportunity to specifically ask the client about any allegations made in the not-yet filed countercomplaint.

To make the most of your interrogatories and save your client some money, you should have your own "form interrogatories." For example, you can keep a document of interrogatories that are separated by specific category. Rather than by just "physical custody," "legal custody," and "child

---

[1] USCS Fed Rules Civ Proc R 33(1)(a).

[2] West's Annotated Code of Maryland, Maryland Rules, Title 2. Civil Procedure–Circuit Court Form Interrogatories (Refs & Annos), Form No. 5- DOMESTIC RELATIONS INTERROGATORIES.

support," have them organized by specific high-conflict topics as well. For example, if the opposing party believes your client should have supervised access, then you should have at least one interrogatory that deals with this issue. An example of this is:

> "If you believe the other parent's access should be supervised, include the name, address, and phone number of any visit supervisors and/or supervised visitation centers that you believe are appropriate. If supervised visitation has already occurred, state the dates and duration, and include the name, address, and phone number of any visit supervisors and/or supervised visitation centers. Attach to your answers any reports in your possession that have been issued by the supervisor."

For child support purposes, if the opposing party owns a business, include questions directed at them as running a business rather than at them as an employee. Other categories that you can separate your interrogatories into are based on common high-conflict issues such as "Domestic Violence, "Co-Parenting," "Withholding Access," "Mental Health," "Substance Abuse," and "Voluntary Impoverishment." This way, when you identify an issue that is case specific, you will have a few interrogatory forms ready to rely on to get the information you need.

In answering interrogatories, get the Word document from opposing counsel. That saves you time you would otherwise spend on converting or retyping their interrogatories. Send your client the Word document and ask that they answer the interrogatories in the document itself right under each interrogatory. Explain to them that they need to answer all parts of each interrogatory, so review each request carefully. The better the client answers the questions, the less time it will take you to revise them. In answering the questions fully, the client is saving you the time you would spend chasing after them for the missing information. Make sure to give them a deadline at least five days before the due date, so that you can review, revise, and format appropriately.

Requests for Admissions of Fact

If Requests for Admissions of Fact (RFAs) are an option in your jurisdiction, please do not overlook this important tool. If you are not familiar with them, RFAs require one of three responses from the opposing party:

"Admit," "Deny," or (if appropriate) "Objection." In some jurisdictions, the option for this method is unlimited. Nevertheless, it is not a tool you have to use every time. It is a tool that can be used when the opposing party has a credibility issue. Unfortunately, we all know too well that clients do not always tell their lawyers the truth. RFAs come in handy if the opposing party is outright lying, and if you have a reasonable basis to believe this. This tool is all about how you can commit them to a statement, and it is where you can really put your client to work. Your client is going to know better what the opposing party is going to lie about, and they can help with drafting out the requests and then editing them. Not only is this a great tool to propound, but it also is fairly easy for your client to respond with the minimal need to edit or revise. The simple admission or denial in response to an RFA makes it an affordable and effective tool for everyone involved.

Both RFAs and Interrogatories are statements under oath. Do not forget the importance of credibility as mentioned at the onset of this chapter. The judge simply will not have an exact picture of what goes on in your client's home or in the opposing party's home. It is rare that they will even meet the child or children about whom they will make life-changing decisions. It is even rarer that they get a full picture of what is really going on in each parent's home. They must rely on the credibility of the litigants. If you can impeach the other side by discovery on a very important issue, you may be on your way to winning your case.

Cases are won and lost on credibility alone. There are clients who have allowed the opposing party to have primary custody for many years before filing for custody. In one case, the client sought legal counsel when his daughter, one of three kids he had together with the opposing party, started refusing to go to his home as they had previously agreed. Flash forward to just days before the client signed off on our proposed settlement agreement. He got a call from his children's mother's former employer letting him know that she alleged to her prior employer that the parties' oldest son had passed away in order to extort money from them for funeral expenses. She went so far as to doctor a fake obituary for the oldest son. To make matters even worse, their oldest (who is very much alive to this day) was the child she was agreeing would be in the primary custody of the client. Although the case was very close to conclusion, after careful discussion of the options and an explanation that a modification would require the event to occur after the most recent court order, the client agreed it was best to fight. It was far too late in the proceedings to get a mental health expert or custody evaluator to correlate her underlying issues with her fitness as a parent. The strategy became showing that the defendant had no regard for the truth, and therefore, her testimony could not be trusted. A well-developed settlement had to be relinquished, but fortunately, in the end, the court agreed with the opinion regarding credibility. In contrast, the testimony of the client, who was completely forthright on the stand and had been a fair and reasonable co-parent throughout, was used as testament of his integrity and character. In the end, the client was awarded primary custody of all three of his children, including his daughter, who had not been in his care in almost a year. Credibility for the large majority of family law cases, especially when there are no resources to have experts testify, will make or break your case. The judge needs to rely on your client's word and weigh it against the other party's word to see who is more credible. It frequently becomes a literal "he said/she said" dispute, even though a lack of credibility may not speak to either party's fitness as a parent. Using the tools of discovery to discredit the other side is what shows to the judge that they should trust the word of one party over the other.

REQUESTS FOR PRODUCTION OF DOCUMENTS

Requests for Production of Documents are among the most pertinent discovery tools. There is a special amount of information that you can get from these documents that you cannot get from any other documents in any other part of discovery. Even if it is just the most basic information, you can use that information to get the information you need, even if it is not provided.

It can be hard to resist the urge to become giddy when looking through bank and credit card statements. How a person spends their money is endlessly useful information: for instance, if the other side seems to be living beyond their means, bank statements will shed light as to any gift or undeclared income. Additionally, if there are issues with alcohol abuse, you can look through their statements to find liquor store or bar charges and highlight their frequency in cross-examination. Bank statements will also tell you what credit cards they hold, in the event they didn't provide any or all of their credit card statements. Make sure to pay particular attention to what account their pay statements are deposited in. Usually, pay statements will have the last four digits of the account that the payment is directly deposited into. As you jot down your notes on bank and credit card statements, make sure each account has at least its last four digits written down. This helps at the conclusion of reviewing the discovery provided, because you can make note of all the accounts accounted for versus what has been provided to you.

Document production is going to require your client to put in legwork anyway, so make it as easy as possible for them to produce the documents in a manner that will require the least amount of compilation and action on your part. Explain to the client the ways in which they can get the commonly requested documents online. Even if they do not already have an online account for their financial documents, bills, and the child's records, encourage them to create a login. Tax records can be requested through the Internal Revenue Service website as well as Social Security Earnings Histories. For text messages, call logs, or photos from their phone, recommend that they use reliable backup software. It does not require much effort other than the client backing up their phone through a computer. This software will allow them to download the entire text message correspondence into one document, so they do not have to take hundreds of screenshots in a photo format and you do not have to discern the order. Texts from the backup are also more reliable in providing the exact dates and time for each text, making them far better evidence than the screenshots.

Once the client has compiled the records, have them put a cover sheet with the number of the request in front of the corresponding documents, or, in the alternative, save the document with the request number in the title. It is easier to receive the documents in bulk if you use a large file share program like Google Drive or Dropbox. Send the client the Word version of the other side's document requests and have them write in response under each individual request as to what they have in their possession or control. That will require less time for you to figure out what is missing and to draft the written responses. Be sure to include standard objections at the beginning of the written responses, such as objecting to the production of any documents beyond the past three years, to cover all your bases at trial.

Regardless of which discovery tool you are using, remember to review your client's responses. Always review and revise (with approval) your client's interrogatories. But it's important to review and make note of their responses to document requests and RFAs. You may learn new information that will require a strategy discussion with your client.

REQUESTING SOCIAL MEDIA DATA IN DISCOVERY

These days, you may be missing out on some major evidence if you do not include social media in your discovery requests. You can certainly get information off of public profiles and Google searches, but there are a lot more benefits to collecting the entirety of the opposing party's data.

A 2010 survey by the American Academy of Matrimonial Lawyers found that Facebook makes up 66 percent of primary source divorce evidence. When conducting the requests for production of documents, never forget to ask for the downloaded data from the opposing party's Facebook account. This data will include the person's friend list, posts, comments, private messages, and groups they belong to, among other information. To this end, the following is standard language for requesting Facebook data:

> *If you have a Facebook account, an electronic copy of your Facebook data. (To obtain a copy of your Facebook data, complete the following steps: 1. Go to* ***Facebook****.com/settings. 2. Tap "****Download*** *a copy of your* ***Facebook data.****" 3. Tap "****Download Archive.****" 4. It might take a few minutes, but* ***Facebook*** *will alert you when your* ***archive*** *is ready. 5. When it is, click "****Download Archive****" again, and a zip file will* ***download*** *to your computer. (The result is an electronic file which should be provided to the propounding attorney in electronic form.)*[3]

Keep in mind, however, that these instructions do change from time to time with Facebook. Facebook data tends to be the most fruitful and is a gold mine of information to use in the litigation of child custody. While it is time consuming, going through all the opposing party's Facebook messages is well worth it. An example of this would be a parent using their Facebook to sell their prescription pills to various contacts (true story). In one case, messages were found between the opposing party and her live-in boyfriend, who the client believed was physically abusing their son. The message indicated that he beat her son to discipline him. Messages were also found between the opposing party and a friend, which revealed that at the onset of the

---

[3] Valerie E. Anias, *How to Obtain a Copy of a Client's Complete Facebook History*, Practice Points, May 25, 2017. https://www.americanbar.org/groups/litigation/committees/family-law/practice/2017/how-to-obtain-a-copy-of-facebook-history/.

custody case, she planned on taking the child and moving out of state without a word.

Since social media platforms are always changing, be sure to keep in the loop of what is used. This way, you can cite specific examples of apps in your document requests. A good way to stay on top of what is popular is asking around and, also, looking for the most popular apps in the App Store or the Google Play store. Look specifically under the Lifestyle Apps categories. Be sure to look out for apps that involve messaging (e.g., WhatsApp, Snapchat), dating apps (e.g., Tinder, Bumble, Grindr, and Hinge), and video doorbells (e.g., Ring, Nest), payment apps (e.g., Venmo, CashApp), and look in apps that allow you to hide photos or messages with the appearance of being an ordinary app such as a calculator, calendar, or to-do list by searching "hidden vault."

USING PUBLIC PROFILES AND INTERNET SEARCHES FOR EVIDENCE

Beyond the apps and Facebook, make sure you ask for a variety of other social media website profiles. Many times, you will be able to review an opposing party's social media accounts at the onset of your case, if they do not have the appropriate privacy settings. This is something you should ask your client right away: does the opposing party have and use social media? The sooner you can get access to any public profile, the quicker you can save their profile and any other posts before they claim they do not have a profile. If your jurisdiction has a public court records search, also make sure to search the opposing party's name as soon you open the case. You never know what criminal charges you may find that your client didn't know or tell you about.

Many lawyers have had luck with just doing a Google search. In one case, the other party's job history was procured through finding her resume on Indeed. She claimed she only had some past job experience in real estate. As it turns out, she was a certified dental assistant. This search provided the name of the office she was most recently employed at in order to subpoena her pay information. In a divorce case, a hidden asset was found by searching the VIN number on a classic car that the client's husband had allegedly sold. Public auction records revealed that he sold it to himself through his business entity. Google, and a follow-up search through land records, helped find an opposing party's new address when the private investigator who was hired to do a skip trace on her could not find her address. These are just a few examples.

SUBPOENAS

Subpoenas with the necessary accompanying documents for initial discovery are crucial. In some jurisdictions, you need a Notice of Records Deposition for any records needed within the discovery period. These are great to use when you know right away if the opposing party is lying about their income, if they aren't going to give you any of their health records, or if they have already tried in some way to prevent your client from getting the children's school or medical records. This makes for great proof that there has been an attempt of one parent to alienate the other from the child's life. For mental health records, you will likely need a Health Insurance Portability and Accountability Act (HIPAA) waiver. You can make a motion asking the court to compel disclosure, as the mental health of a parent is pertinent to their parental fitness. Be sure to subpoena financial records that the opposing party has not provided. Please keep in mind that if you are asking for three years or more back, that is not documentation that can be easily pulled through online banking. Getting every check copy is not easy either. The best way to get these documents, especially if you are trying to go far back, is to subpoena them, rather than hound the other side for them. You get a much fuller picture of the other party's finances, without their interference. Additionally, you get the benefit of ensuring that you will have a certificate of the records' custodian in order to make them self-authenticating documents.

CONCLUSION

Discovery is an essential aspect of litigation. When you use all of your options and tailor your requests to the facts of the case at hand, you maximize your chances for success.

6

Dealing with the Unrepresented Opposing Party

Having to deal with an unrepresented opposing party is unavoidable when you represent clients of modest means. This does not have to be a contentious and unnecessarily prolonged proceeding. The tips listed in this chapter will provide the mindset for working cooperatively with the self-represented opposition in a way that effectively advances the case.

In bringing or defending a custody case, a party may choose not to hire a lawyer and to represent himself or herself instead. Such unrepresented parties are known as *pro se* litigants. Given that most *pro se* litigants are not lawyers and do not understand court procedures or evidentiary rules, litigating a case against a *pro se* litigant can be difficult and costly. However, an awareness of the unique challenges posed by *pro se* proceedings can help attorneys minimize such difficulties and associated litigation costs. A number of strategies that attorneys may find helpful in accomplishing this goal are discussed here.

STATE CLEARLY YOUR ROLE TO THE *PRO SE* LITIGANT

In every correspondence made to a *pro se* litigant, it is essential for your protection that you communicate first in writing and establish who you represent. Make it clear that you are writing with the understanding that they are not represented. A sample of this, which can be included at the start of all written correspondence with a *pro se* litigant: "I am writing this under the understanding that you have not gotten a lawyer to represent you in this matter. If you have an attorney, do not respond directly to me or my office. Instead, forward this correspondence to your attorney and have them respond to me directly."

In the course of the custody matter, a *pro se* opponent may ask you what they should do. In responding to these kinds of questions, you should and must be very careful not to violate any ethical rules. Model Rule 4.3 provides:[1]

> *Transactions with Persons Other than Clients*
>
> ***In dealing on behalf of a client with a person who is not represented by counsel, a lawyer shall not state or imply that the lawyer is disinterested. When the lawyer knows or reasonably should know that the unrepresented person misunderstands the lawyer's role in the matter, the lawyer shall make reasonable efforts to correct the misunderstanding. The lawyer shall not give legal advice to an unrepresented person, other than the advice to secure counsel, if the lawyer knows or reasonably should know that the interests of such a person are or have a reasonable possibility of being in conflict with the interests of the client.***

Be sure to explain to a *pro se* party that you only owe a duty to your client and that you will always be acting in the best interests of your client. The only "advice" you can give in this situation with the *pro se* party is that they should seek and/or hire legal counsel of their own. Following this advice, you should be protected from this rule and misunderstandings later.

---

[1] Center for Professional Responsibility, American Bar Association, Model Rules of Professional Conduct (2020).

EXPLAIN THE ACTIONS YOU ARE TAKING

While you must avoid giving the *pro se* opposing party legal advice, you can minimize frustrations in the case. By writing letters, emails, and other communications explaining your actions to the *pro se* litigant, you may be able to make the litigation process less mysterious to them and thereby reduce the chances that the *pro se* litigant will file unnecessary pleadings. You may also be gently guiding them toward meeting your client in towards an amicable resolution that promotes your client's desires. If you take a scorched-earth policy dealing with the unrepresented side, you will only increase the amount of court time for the case.

REMAIN PROFESSIONAL WITH THE *PRO SE* LITIGANT

In the course of dealing with a *pro se* litigant, remain professional. This individual already does not trust you. You are viewed as the enemy in this case. Being polite can be difficult when the *pro se* litigant is yelling and calling you names. Always use "sir" and "ma'am" along with Mr./Ms. when you address them. You are setting the tone for how you handle them. The respect may be reciprocated in your dealings with them, making the litigation less contentious.

Remaining cool and calm in dealing with a *pro se* litigant can minimize the litigation and even circumvent any retaliatory actions by the *pro se* party against you personally. *Pro se* litigants are more inclined to file a grievance with the state bar against attorneys who treated them poorly. By losing your calm demeanor, you can let your own emotions govern and lose sight of advocating for your client as an objective lawyer.

AVOID LEGAL JARGON IF POSSIBLE

Try to use layperson's language whenever possible. If a delay can be stated as "postponing the date" instead of the legal term of "continuance," try to use the nonlegal language. Calling someone a "pro per" may sound derogatory, if not elitist, so refer to the opposing party as "representing yourself." If a disclosure statement or settlement letter cites the law, include a copy of the statute. Asking the self-represented litigant to "provide disclosure in accordance with Rule XYZ of the Court Rules" can be better stated as "We are required under the local court rules to exchange bank statements and other information so we each have the other's information." Your court system (self-service center or website) may provide lists of documents to be exchanged in family cases, and providing a court-generated document or list may look more official and less arbitrary than the attorney's letter demanding (or even politely requesting) the same documents.

SEEK THE ASSISTANCE OF THE JUDGE EARLY

As soon as possible, ask the court in your case to set a case status hearing. Use this court appearance to ask the judge for straightforward instructions about the exchange of financial and other required information and how the case will proceed, including future court dates. This is also an opportunity to have the court discuss the benefits of mediation or other alternative dispute resolution processes.

Family court judges are accustomed to having self-represented litigants in court and will appreciate that your case includes an attorney who is conscientious and respectful of the process. Use the initial status conference experience to enhance the self-represented party's opinion of attorneys and the court system. Using this method further expedites the entire litigation, because it has the court setting deadlines and court dates. The case will not fall between the cracks and sit stale for months. Your client will likely appreciate this method of keeping the case moving more quickly.

TRY TO RESOLVE ISSUES WITH A *PRO SE* LITIGANT BEFORE SEEKING THE COURT'S INTERVENTION

In a highly contested custody case involving a *pro se* litigant, you, understandably, may be tempted to file a motion asking the court to sanction the *pro se* litigant for failing to comply with court rules or discovery. However, before filing such a motion, carefully consider whether it is the most effective and smartest means of resolving the particular issue. Oftentimes, the judge may be sympathetic to the *pro se* party, even when you are technically correct. The result? You may win your motion hearing and not receive any of the requested relief unless the behavior is repeated. Write letters and call the opposing side to attempt to resolve the issue. Document every attempt to resolve the matter prior to asking the judge to resolve the issue. The documented attempts will show you have done everything possible prior to bringing the motion.

DO NOT TAKE THEM LIGHTLY

While many *pro se* litigants have little experience with the law or court, others do have litigation experience or spend substantial amounts of time researching the law. Keep in mind these individuals have all day every day to dedicate to their case. We do not have such luxury. Simply put, do not assume the *pro se* party will be an easy case you can just show up and win. A *pro se* litigant who was represented by a lawyer early in the case may even have pleadings they may revise and file in the case requiring your response. These pleadings and motions may include well-supported and articulate arguments with persuasive case law. Some *pro se* litigants will go to the courthouse and print pleadings from well-known family law attorneys to use as their own. We must remember that the opposing party is their own lawyer. Treat them as a lawyer and prepare as required.

UNDERSTAND THE RISKS OF NEGOTIATING WITH A *PRO SE* LITIGANT

In the course of settlement negotiations, a *pro se* party can mischaracterize statements made by you or your client. To avoid this issue, whenever possible, have another person present as a witness to settlement negotiations with a *pro se* party. Ideally, that witness should be a third-party neutral familiar with the court process, such as a mediator, a parenting coordinator, or a Guardian Ad Litem. When a parenting coordinator or a Guardian Ad Litem is involved, try to include them so they can weigh in on any disputes. A reasonable position will sound far better to the *pro se* litigant when it is coming from a neutral professional rather than you.

If possible, keep all communications in writing. Even if they call you, let it go to voicemail (keep the voicemail if possible) or take the call and promptly obtain their email address. Set boundaries by telling *pro se* litigants that you will only communicate with them in writing to avoid any miscommunications. If you choose to speak to the opposing party via telephone, always follow up with an email recapping the oral conversation as documentation in the event your credibility is questioned. At the end of every written communication with a *pro se* litigant, be sure to reiterate that you represent only your client's interests and to recommend that they should seek the advice of counsel of their own choosing. You may also want to remind your client, if they are copied on communications, that it is better for settlement negotiations when the other side has the advice of counsel to set their expectations.

Further, after a settlement has been reached with a *pro se* litigant, the individual may later claim—honestly or not—that there was a misunderstanding as to the terms of the settlement and, accordingly, that no agreement was reached. To minimize such risks, an attorney should ensure that any agreed-upon settlement terms are promptly memorialized in writing and signed by both parties. For instance, if a settlement is reached through a mediation, both parties should sign a written summary of the settlement terms before the mediation concludes. Alternatively, if a court hearing results in a settlement, an attorney may ask to have the settlement terms placed on the record to bind the parties and ensure no misunderstandings.

CONCLUSION

Dealing directly with a *pro se* party can be difficult and nerve-wracking from an ethical standpoint. Unfortunately, it is inevitable with parties that come from modest means. To protect yourself, keep communications in writing or in front of a third party. To protect your client's financial interests, make your role clear to the *pro se* party, explain that you cannot give them legal advice, and recommend they seek counsel of their own selection. This will lower the chances of the *pro se* party calling or emailing you over every minor disagreement they have with your client.

7

Explore and Develop Options for Finding Low-Cost (Necessary) Professionals

In situations that give rise to a potential risk of harm to the child, child custody cases need an expert. What do you do when your client does not have thousands of dollars to shell out for a custody evaluator, Guardian Ad Litem, or child psychologist? Without the intervention of such experts, a judge may not be able to identify indicators of serious abuse, neglect, or parental alienation. This chapter is dedicated to giving you ideas on how to get the expert information without breaking the client's bank.

DO YOU NEED AN EXPERT?

The first question you should ask yourself is whether you actually need an expert. Sometimes we as attorneys can tailor the argument and presentation of the case to cover the necessary information for the court to consider without the need for an expert in the field. The first step would be to do your own research on the topic for the case. Read journals in that particular field so that you're better educated for this particular topic.

Should you feel that after all your time researching a particular topic, you need this topic evaluated in your child custody case, it is time to find your expert.

SHOP AROUND

This should come as no shock to you: Do not go with the "usual" expert in your court system. Too often, this expert may charge top-dollar fees for their services. Instead, look for the up-and-coming star in your area. This will take some research on your part. If you have the good fortune of living in a town with a university or college, call the institution in which these experts would study. The institution may have some ideas/referrals for your case and usually love referring work to their alumni.

Also consider using the expert who is just beginning their practice, perhaps under the supervision of a high-dollar/more experienced expert in the field. They will usually charge much less than the supervisor, but you can rest assured they are usually doing good work under the supervision of the experienced supervisor. Of course, you should not neglect doing your due diligence on the up-and-coming star expert. Interview them via telephone at a minimum to ensure their personality and presentation will be welcomed by the judge in your matter. Interview the expert to ensure your expectations are understood and can be met. A little homework on your part here will possibly save you the headache of an incomplete and/or poor evaluation when it comes time for a final custody hearing.

ASK FOR A FLAT FEE FOR SERVICES

When you are investigating an expert for possible hire, always request a flat-fee quote and what the fee covers or doesn't cover. Try to limit any surprises for later as best you can on the cost. The client will appreciate a flat-fee expert so they can budget accordingly to hire an expert at all. The client may be able to get a loan from family/friends for the expert if they know what it will cost. Even the court-appointed experts will charge a flat fee for the costs of their investigation. You may also want to find out well in advance what they charge to testify. If you need them at trial, it's better to prepare your client so that they can save up for the expert's fees.

Alternatively, if you have an evergreen retainer structure, you pay the fees directly through their balance with your office.

> *Cost Savings Tip*: **Be sure to inform the expert that you're taking this case for a reduced fee. The expert may be more sympathetic on the cost of their services and give your client a break on fees.**

EXPERT WITNESS DIRECTORY

Research using an expert directory that lists individuals for virtually any topic that you may need an expert for in that field. The directories are free to the consumer, and you can search by topic. Once you search that particular field, you can review the actual individuals' educational backgrounds, work history, any published works by the individual, and (as some provide) their hourly rate. These are typically available in both print and electronic versions for consumers.

CONSIDER HIRING AN EXPERT FOR INSTRUCTIONAL TESTIMONY

Consider hiring an expert for an hour or two of their time to come to the trial for the sole purpose of explaining an issue for the court. The expert would not assess the parties, the child in the case, and/or any reports personal to the case at hand. Their only role would be to educate the court on an issue such as parental alienation. Have them address what is typically required for assessments and in behavior for the issue at hand. If the court can become more educated on an issue, the direct examination and cross-examination of the parties may tie directly to the instructional testimony and thus advocate the theory of your side.

THE PARENT'S OWN THERAPIST

Should your client already be in therapy for any mental health issues they may be facing, consider bringing the therapist to discuss the parent's progress. The parent's therapist may have built a good rapport with your client and might not charge an outrageous amount for their testimony. This would be beneficial if your client is accused of having an issue with managing their anger. The parent's therapist can dispel this allegation with relatively little difficulty. This does not mean you shouldn't investigate the therapist to learn their credentials and to ensure they are the right kind of therapist to answer questions on the appropriate topic: A therapist who is trained with anger management may not have the credentials to assess addiction issues, and vice versa.

ASSESS THE COSTS AT COURT

Should the other side have more financial resources than your client, request at a preliminary hearing that the court assess the costs against the higher earner or in a higher percentage. The court could later reassess these costs at any final trial to reimburse the other parent. Make it known to the court that the expert is necessary in the case and that financial resources should not be a bar when there is a risk of harm to a child.

USE TREATISES

Sometimes the information you need doesn't come from an actual warm body in the witness chair. Consider joining the Association of Family and Conciliation Courts or other similar organizations. These organizations have databases with articles written by experts in the respective fields you are seeking. The database contains multiple guides for attorneys and clients dealing with a wide variety of topics including parental alienation, child development and attachment, and how to cross-examine for intimate partner violence, etc. Consider tailoring your direct and cross-examination questioning to the topics in the articles and offering the article as a treatise under your local evidence rules. The more you can connect the witness questioning to the respective expert publication, the more persuasive your argument appears to the judge in the case. This can address your necessary information from an expert at a very low (or no) cost for the client.

CONSIDER AN EXPERT CONSULTATION

Another possible approach in your case may be to have a consultation with the expert to be better educated for the issues at hand. The expert may charge a small fee for a consultation as many of us do, but it will be much less than the cost of a full evaluation. The consultation will give you the opportunity to learn more about the topic at hand, have the expert give you the procedures that he/she would use if retained, and may direct you to their preferred resources for your own reading and introduction as a possible treatise.

Should you go down this road, draft all of the questions you may have prior to the meeting. Come prepared to make the most of your consultation with the professional. You can also use this opportunity to make a new friend who could be beneficial to future clients.

WHERE POSSIBLE, STIPULATE!

Aside from narrowing down the statement of facts for a trial, if you can get opposing counsel and/or the judge to take judicial notice to the stipulation of issues such as "domestic violence causes trauma for children," you do not need to have an expert testify to this issue. Work with the other side prior to any and all hearings/trials to set forth for the court what the parties actually agree upon. You may be surprised to learn what you can get stipulated. The judges will appreciate reducing the issues and specialized knowledge at hand for the court.

COURT-APPOINTED EXPERTS

If your jurisdiction provides the option for an expert appointed by the court, they are more often than not far cheaper than a privately hired expert. Court-appointed experts are often custody evaluators or forensic psychologists. If the court has its own staff custody evaluator or forensic psychologist, this service could be free of charge. Alternatively, the court may offer a fee waiver for indigent clients or split the costs in proportion to each party's percent of their combined income. If you have to file a motion for the appointment of an expert, make sure to request who should be responsible for the fees or how you want the costs to be divided between the parties.

There is a large advantage to using an expert appointed by the court in that the court may deem this expert the "court's expert" and will reasonably rely on their recommendations. An expert hired by you runs the risk of looking like a hired gun and could be slaughtered on the stand for his or her bias by opposing counsel.

The court-appointed custody evaluator is typically a social worker who will meet with or go to the homes of both parties and observe the interactions between each parent and child. It is crucial to prepare your client for the custody evaluation in order to get the best results out of the evaluation. This is the best way to avoid an unfavorable report. You can do a mock interview with them with questions a custody evaluator might ask. Remind them to keep the focus on the child. It is essential not to completely trash the other party or bring up minor petty incidents between the two of them. Ask them to name strengths and weaknesses of the other parents in your mock interview, so they will not be scratching their head or be without an answer when it comes time for the actual interview. The evaluator may ask your client to provide references or documents supporting their position. Speak with them beforehand about potential references. It is important to have someone who has actually seen your client as a parent, not just someone who can only attest to their character. Make sure that they are familiarized with their child's teachers, medical providers, and extracurricular coaches or instructors. The custody evaluator may speak to any one of these individuals or get records from them. It is best to look at beforehand or provide directly any documents for the evaluator's review: you never know when the client may think something is helpful that actually does more harm than good for them. You most likely are not privy to the discussions with the custody evaluator. Instruct your client to tell you if they voluntarily want to communicate with the custody evaluator afterwards. This prevents your client from disclosing unfavorable evidence.

Even if the custody evaluation is not favorable to your client, the report of the evaluator can be used to reach a fair settlement. Explain to your client about the court's reliance on this expert and the likelihood that the court will order exactly what the report recommends. You may be able to negotiate a deal with the other side that is better than the evaluator's recommendations so that both parties avoid the high costs of going to trial.

USEFUL EXPERTS

Mental Health

Untreated mental illnesses are a typical underlying current in contested family law cases. Make sure that you ask your client about any concerning behaviors of the opposing party, history of problems with substance abuse, and any fear of harm against themselves, their children, or others. A mental health expert provides specific insight as to how mental illness can create an impediment to parental fitness and what can be done to minimize the impact on the children.

In cases where one of the parties is already undergoing mental health treatment, using their authenticated treatment records may be a cheaper alternative. They may be willing to produce their treatment records, or you can get a court order to have the records released by the provider or mandate the party to waive privilege. This would allow you to get the party's diagnosis, treatment plan, statements concerning potential risk of harm, and to verify compliance with the plan and medications. This could be advantageous if you already spoke with the provider and do not believe they would make a good witness. In the alternative, it may be a disadvantage if you are faced with complex medical terms or illegible notes in the records you choose to put into evidence. The lay witness will not be able to explain these, and it could call into question the probative value of the evidence.

In cases where the child is in treatment, it may be useful to use the child's therapist, provided privilege has been waived. The child's therapist can provide professional insight into the child's behavior, the possibility of alienation, and any concerning information they may have learned about. Before using a child's therapist, find out which parent hired the therapist, what each parent's involvement was in selecting the therapist, what the therapist's qualifications are, who is paying for the therapist, and how much contact the therapist has had with each parent. The therapist may not be worthwhile if there is too much undue influence from the other parent. However, these considerations will come in handy in cross-examination if the child's therapist is called by the other side.

Private Investigator

Since it is difficult to find out what is going on in a child's other home, the use of a private investigator may be necessary. In my child custody cases, I have suggested the use of a private investigator when a client alleges their children are being left with a third party, or even unsupervised, during the other parent's custody time. A private investigator can be used to show this type of neglect as well as potential substance abuse and domestic disputes occurring in the home.

It is very difficult to prove what is going on in the home of the other party. Private investigators can help with suspicions your client may have about the child being repeatedly left in the care of a third party or being left home alone, and they can even help with identifying alcohol abuse. For instance, having a private investigator follow the other party might show how often that party takes trips to the liquor store when they have the child. If a client expresses these concerns without having the evidence needed for their case, having the client hire a private investigator before filing for custody allows you to better provide them with cost-benefit analysis of their claims.

PARENTING COORDINATOR

After a court has issued a parenting arrangement for the parties (temporary or permanent), the tension and issues likely do not cease overnight. Hiring a parenting coordinator is one way to potentially alleviate those tensions and assist in the custody matter. The parenting coordinator can assist the parents in their co-parenting in different ways, including facilitating communication between the parties. They can further this assistance by educating the parents on communication techniques where they may fail otherwise.

The parenting coordinator can usually keep tensions down and help further the best interest of the child. The coordinator typically will meet the child at least once to assess how stressed he/she is at the time. They can then take this assessment to the child's therapist, if any, to address with the child in therapy.

Check to see if your state has a statute setting forth the requirements of a parenting coordinator. Most require the parenting coordinator to have at least a master's degree and have some specialized training, including domestic violence. The North Carolina statute states:[1]

> (a) To be eligible to be included on the district court's list of parenting coordinators, a person must meet all of the following requirements:
> (1) Hold a masters or doctorate degree in psychology, law, social work, counseling, medicine, or a related subject area.

---

[1] N.C. GEN STAT. § 50–93 (2020).

(2) Have at least five years of related professional post-degree experience.
(3) Hold a current license in the parenting coordinator's area of practice, if applicable.
(4) Participate in 24 hours of training in topics related to the developmental stages of children, the dynamics of high-conflict families, the stages and effects of divorce, problem solving techniques, mediation, and legal issues.

(b) In order to remain eligible as a parenting coordinator, the person must also attend parenting coordinator seminars that provide continuing education, group discussion, and peer review and support.

Keeping the tensions down through the use of a parenting coordinator should lower the odds you end up in multiple hearings on the same kind of issue and avoid further litigation through contempt and modification actions. The parties also may behave if they feel they are being monitored by a potential witness for court. You should also warn your client that communications with the parenting coordinator are not covered by confidentiality.

Lastly, the parenting coordinator does not usually make any custody recommendations. This is one of the major differences between a parenting coordinator and a Guardian Ad Litem. The coordinator will, however, address concerns he/she has with the court, including a parent's behavior, statements made by the parties and/or the child, and any other needs that the coordinator may witness. The coordinator could be the unbiased witness your case may need and at a cheaper rate than a Guardian Ad Litem or other evaluators.

JUVENILE COURT REFERRAL

In Georgia and some other jurisdictions, transferring the contested child custody portion of a divorce to a juvenile court may be an option and very beneficial. This is advantageous because the juvenile court could appoint experts, including a Guardian Ad Litem or custody evaluator, and could provide a setting for mediation. The court may compensate the experts and cost the parties absolutely nothing. Explore your jurisdiction and your court rules and judge's preferences and find out whether this is an option if your case is a divorce with contested child custody. The Virginia statute states:[2]

§ 16.1-244. Concurrent jurisdiction; exceptions.

A. Nothing contained in this law shall deprive any other court of the concurrent jurisdiction to determine the custody of children upon a writ of habeas corpus under the law, or to determine the custody, guardianship, visitation or support of children when such custody, guardianship, visitation or support is incidental to the determination of causes pending in such courts, nor deprive a circuit court of jurisdiction to determine spousal support in a suit for separate maintenance. However, when a suit for divorce has been filed in a circuit court, in which the custody, guardianship, visitation or support of children of the parties or spousal support is raised by the pleadings and a hearing, including a pendente lite hearing, is set by the circuit court on any such issue for a date certain or on a motions docket to be heard within 21 days of the filing, the juvenile and domestic relations district courts shall be divested of the right to enter any further decrees or orders to determine custody, guardianship, visitation or support when raised for such hearing and such matters shall be determined by the circuit court unless both parties agreed to a referral to the juvenile court. Nothing in this section shall deprive a circuit court of the authority to refer any such case to a commissioner for a hearing or shall deprive the juvenile and domestic relations district courts of the jurisdiction to enforce its valid orders prior to the entry of a conflicting order of any circuit court for any period during which the order was in effect or to temporarily place a child in the custody of any person when that child has been adjudicated abused, neglected, in need of services or delinquent subsequent to the order of any circuit court.

CHILD'S SCHOOL COUNSELOR

Be careful subpoenaing the child's counselor for the contested child custody matter. They typically hate getting involved. They also may be of little use in the matter. Assess whether they are necessary in the matter. If by chance you

---

[2] Va. Code § 16.1-244 (2022).

do believe they can provide a benefit to your trial strategy, discuss the matter with them prior. Inform them of what you are seeking in their testimony. If they are reluctant to come to court, ask if they would write an affidavit to state what you are seeking in writing. If an affidavit will not hold up in your jurisdiction, ask them for any notes or records they keep in the ordinary course of the counseling sessions. Ask for them with a records certification.

CONCLUSION

The tips given in this chapter will give you some avenues to get the expert testimony for your case that you may have otherwise thought was a dead end. They have stood the test of time in getting the necessary information with limited funds. You may need to be creative on how you can get the expert information and/or evaluation admitted, but these experts can go a long way toward resolving the case and avoiding the high costs of litigation.

CONCLUSIONS

8

Techniques for Settling at Mediation

Many states now require mediation prior to scheduling a final hearing on the issues. This chapter is about how to better coach your client to have an open mind at mediation to get a settlement at this stage and minimize litigation. It will explain how to narrow down the issues, be creative in the settlement process, and shorten the mediation process to reduce costs.

MEET BEFOREHAND

In the week prior to mediation, send the client options for potential settlements in the matter to see what they might be open to. Request a meeting or phone call to discuss the options once they have seen them written out. This meeting is the ideal time to be real with clients about what their chances are, what you believe is reasonable, and when mediation may be a lost cause.

Take this opportunity to explain the setup of mediation and what the role of the mediator is. In some jurisdictions, attorneys are not invited to take part in custody mediation; it is just the parties and the mediator. In that case you may want to explain the decorum of the mediation and the inadmissibility of these settlement discussions. Explain that the mediator is not a judge and that nothing is binding until it is approved and signed. Let them know there will be no evidence taken, and that they are not to bring any with them. The client must understand that arguing or getting heated with the other parent is not helpful in mediation and will only move them further away from a resolution.

ESTABLISH A BOTTOM LINE

It is important to know exactly what your client will be willing to settle for going into the mediation. This may be a difficult conversation to have, but if mediation will do more harm than good, the expense of mediation may not be worth it. Consider what topic(s) the parties are too far apart on in their positions (e.g., when both parties ask for primary custody when they live far apart). Also reiterate to the client they are not forced to settle at mediation. This will help reduce the chances of a client later claiming that they were pressured into a mediation settlement. State clearly to the client that they control the mediation settlement process and if they do not feel comfortable settling their matter, they may end the process without harm.

Settle on Smaller Issues

Narrowing issues on topics that are not as contentious can help with reducing the costs of preparation and appearance at trial. Here are a few issues that you may be able to get an agreement on, even if you can't resolve the major issues.

Legal Custody

If the parties cooperatively made decisions before they split up, joint legal custody may be an easy concession. These parents will generally have the same attitude toward the major decisions. Make sure your client knows and understands that this is with regard to long-range decisions, not day-to-day decisions. Many parents think that this gives the other parent control over what happens with the child during their time, so their impulse is to want sole legal custody rather than joint legal custody.

Holidays

Alternating holidays between the parties are an easy agreement, and something judges don't necessarily include in their custody orders. Assess what holidays are important to your client. If they don't celebrate Christmas, you can use that as leverage to get time for the holidays that are important or for more vacation time in the summer. If the parties can agree upon each parent receiving a week or two in the summer, make sure there is a date when the parents are required to inform the other of the designated summer weeks. Be sure to include a provision that gives each party a priority over the other in the event they pick the same weeks, such as mom getting priority in even years and dad getting priority in odd years.

Relocation

No parent wants to be in the position of suddenly having their child move with the other parent out of state or far away. Even if they have to file for emergency custody, it is still a nightmare to have to go to the other state and get that emergency order enforced. Agreeing on how far each party can move with the child can help prevent this from happening. Do not forget to put language that both parents will inform the other of any change in their physical address in the event of relocation. If domestic violence is a point of issue in your custody case, however, you should first assess whether the disclosure of a party's address may do more harm than good.

Right of First Refusal

If the one parent is going to be out of town during their access, there is no reason for the child to be left alone with a babysitter, a significant other, or extended family, if the other parent is available. A mutual right of first refusal is an easy win for both parties. This is another thing that may be left out by a judge's order. Agreeing upon this will actually make co-parenting easier and will give both parties what they want the most: more quality time with their child. A good piece of advice here would be to make the right of refusal for a significant amount of time, such as when the other party is out overnight. If written with language that requires the right of first refusal after only a couple of hours, the parent with the child may not be able to work their job without calling the other parent. This would lead to litigation far too early. At minimum, consider a length of time that exceeds 12 hours. This covers most occupations.

Non-Disparagement

Not disparaging the other parent to the child is also an easy sell. It is certainly helpful in high-conflict cases. One or both parents may be so tied to their own emotions about the other parent that they do not even see how they are affecting their child. If they cannot agree on this, they aren't putting their child's best interest first. Be sure to be as specific as possible so each parent understands that certain actions are not appropriate. Things like asking the child to deliver a message or a child support check are typical. Parents often do not realize how these actions are damaging by placing the child in the middle. A sample of such an agreement:

> Each parent will refrain from exercising undue influence over the child with regard to the other parent, refrain from criticizing the other parent (or that parent's friends or relatives) in the presence of the child, refrain from inducing the child to challenge the authority of the other parent, or encouraging the child to request a change of custody or to resist visitation; neither parent will interrogate the child about the other parent; the parents are to communicate directly with each other concerning the child and will not require the child to deliver messages, including child support payments, to the other parent; the parents will also make their best efforts to prevent third parties from disparaging the parents in the child's presence to the extent that it is possible; both parents shall encourage the child to have a positive relationship with the other parent; the parties shall not discuss issues concerning the child at pickup and drop-off.

Extracurricular Activities

Extracurriculars of the child are also easy to agree upon. Both parents know their child's interests and what activities are most necessary for them. The parties can agree as to who pays for what, who will transport the child, and can agree to allow for both parties to attend the child's games, recitals, or other events. Even if they cannot agree, they can agree to disagree. Each party can have the child enrolled in the activities they choose during their own access only, in which case they can agree that the party should be responsible for the costs also.

Support Issues

Splitting Costs

There are necessary expenses that the parties will incur outside of a support obligation, such as day care or uncovered medical expenses. Present the option of the parties splitting the costs equally. Or in the case of highly disparate incomes, the parties could agree to split these costs in proportion to their percentage of the combined gross income with the higher earner covering the majority. For example, if the parties make a combined income of $100,000 and one party makes $70,000, while the other makes $30,000, suggest a 70/30 split of the expenses.

Health Insurance Coverage

One party is usually covering the child on their health insurance long before the parties go their separate ways. There is no reason for the child to be covered by two policies. In this case, the parties can decide whether the parent covering the child will continue to do so. You can also agree to who would be covering the child if there is a change in employment or coverage of the providing parent, such as the parent with the lower costs for coverage or the better plan.

Access to School and Medical Records

Even if one party has sole legal custody, that does not deprive the other party of the ability to see the child's records. In Maryland, even with sole custody, the custodial parent cannot deny the other parent access to the school and records of the child unless ordered otherwise. This is typically not something that should be denied without a legitimate reason and can be easily agreed upon. Part of the agreement should also include each parent's right to speak directly with the child's educators or medical providers. If the parent with access to this information is denying the other parent the same access, this is a red flag that they are trying to hide something.

CONCLUSION

Even the most contentious cases may have some agreeable middle ground. Don't let a mediation go to waste simply because the parties are too far apart. Try to bring them together on the smaller issues. Draft and sign a partial settlement, if possible. You never know where the spirit of cooperation can take you once the smallest feat has been accomplished.

9

To Depose or Not to Depose

When handling a child custody matter, one discovery tool that may be of use to you is the deposition. Whether or not you actually "need" to use this tool is the question of this chapter. It is important to go over some pros and cons of conducting a deposition for your case. This chapter will conclude with helpful tips should you choose to implement this discovery tool in your case.

PROS OF CONDUCTING A DEPOSITION

Preserving and Locking in Testimony

Depositions are generally the best method for locking in the testimony of unwilling or unfriendly witnesses and the opposing party. Have them tell their testimony without hesitation. Typically, the person is less nervous during the deposition than in a trial court and will be more willing to share a better-detailed version of the story.

Spontaneous Responses

You may elicit more complete and spontaneous answers to questions than with interrogatories you serve in discovery. This is because the witness is far less likely to have rehearsed his/her deposition answers with opposing counsel than when his/her lawyer typed up the interrogatory responses. Depositions are also helpful when witnesses are attempting to be evasive or dodging questions. You can ask the question multiple times in different ways and narrow your line of questioning, resulting in more precise answers.

Evaluating the Witnesses and Opposing Counsel

A deposition lets you see how the other side's witnesses will perform in the witness chair and lets you evaluate whether they will be effective and persuasive with the court. Of course, a stumbling, trembling, and defensive deponent can be transformed into an articulate, confident, and assertive trial witness in part because you gave him a practice session. It also lets you assess the other side's lawyer and whether he/she is competent for any later hearings.

Avoiding Surprises at Trial

Taking the deposition of all witnesses likely to be called by the other side to testify is a great way to be introduced to the testimony that will come out at trial (even the embarrassing items against your client). If some of those witnesses change their stories at trial, you can impeach them with their deposition testimony.

Possibly Settling the Case

Depositions can expose both the strengths and weaknesses of the case for both sides and move the case toward settlement. When deposing the witnesses for the other side, you have a good opportunity to lay out the weaknesses of their case and to "talk" directly to the parent which will influence settlement decisions. The more you can "drill" the other side in a deposition, the less likely are to wish to subject themselves to the treatment again.

CONS OF CONDUCTING A DEPOSITION

Reveals Information to the Other Side

You could lose some advantage by no longer being able to surprise the other side with your line of questioning at trial. They will be more prepared on their case and anticipate some of their probable areas in cross-examination. They could even "fix" some of the items in their life that you have exposed, including passing a drug test. This deposition opens your playbook so you should consider this when deciding to depose.

A "Trial Run"

Witnesses who make a poor showing at the deposition now have the opportunity to refine their ability and skills to be better witnesses at trial. The deposition also provides the witnesses with a dress rehearsal for testifying. It is almost guaranteed that a witness will do better next time, because they know what to expect. By video recording the deposition, you will preserve the testimony and the demeanor of the witness at the dress rehearsal. If it is your witness, you can use this to show them exactly how they can improve. If it's the opposing party's witness, you can use it to prepare your cross examination of them. Check your jurisdiction regarding rules on video depositions. A printed transcript of a deposition does not show the demeanor of the witness the way a video deposition will.

High Cost of Depositions

Considering the time spent preparing for the deposition, taking it, the cost of serving the subpoena, the deposition witness fee, the court reporter's charges, and possible travel expenses, the price is very expensive for our clients. In addition, there is the cost of either summarizing the transcript or of relying on computer programs, not to mention a videographer if the deposition is to be video recorded. Splitting the costs with opposing counsel can save *some* money, but even then, the price remains high. This is the driving factor in deciding whether or not to conduct the deposition. Make sure it is necessary before you schedule it.

Identifying Unknown Witnesses

The lawyer conducting the deposition may alert the other side to the existence and/or importance of a witness unbeknownst to the opposing counsel. For example, if counsel for the defendant decides to take the deposition of the plaintiff's manager on a chance that the boss may know something useful (or for the sake of being thorough), the deposing lawyer may learn that the witness knows much more about the plaintiff's drug habits and the recent occurrence when the plaintiff showed up to work intoxicated. But for taking this deposition, the plaintiff's counsel might never have considered that person as a possible trial witness in a child custody matter.

Opening the Door for Opposing Counsel

Rest assured that if you issue a Notice of Deposition, the next day you will receive one from opposing counsel subjecting your client and others to depositions as well. Once again, consider whether this is an avenue you wish to take.

Now that you have the pros and cons to weigh in deciding whether to conduct a deposition, it is important to know some tips on how to shorten the preparation needed and save money any way you can.

KNOW THE APPLICABLE RULES

When preparing for the deposition, pull your applicable jurisdiction's orders or rules regarding depositions. In some jurisdictions, the court will have the rules that parties must follow posted on its website. Such rules could restrict the duration of the deposition, travel, and even the scope and topic permitted in depositions. Details matter, including the location of the deposition. In Maryland, it is required that the deposition take place in the county where the case is. In short, do your homework if you are going to take a deposition. Lastly, should your jurisdiction have any "standard" rule for deposition stipulations, make sure to look it up. You should copy/paste the stipulations somewhere on your outline in the event that you cannot remember it verbatim, so you can read it onto the record.

THOROUGH INVESTIGATION

When preparing for a deposition, use your investigation skills in uncovering all relevant facts about this particular witness. Social media—discussed in chapter 5—has an abundance of information about a witness's background, memberships in groups and/or clubs, events he/she attends, and interests that can often include information supporting your trial theme. Pictures and comments on social media can sometimes expose embarrassing topics for the witness.

Don't just stop at social media: Find out everything you can about a witness, using the tips listed in chapter 4 for researching the person using public resources. Including all the information you can find against the witness during a deposition can strengthen your case for trial and even potentially push a settlement offer.

Know and Organize Your Documents and Exhibits

In depositions, attorneys often have a stack of documents to go through with the witness as exhibits. You should review and know all the prior-marked documents relevant to the witness being deposed. Read your entire case file, including all pleadings, motions, responses, and statements. The more documents and exhibits you have, the more important it becomes to organize them long before the deposition.

Organize the documents you intend to present to the witness chronologically to match your deposition outline. This will make your deposition of the witness run smoothly and give the impression to the witness that you are adequately prepared for the line of questioning. The more you organize in the days leading up to the deposition, the more information you are likely to pull from a witness in a shorter time.

Use Your Outline Wisely

Your deposition outline should be used as a guide throughout the entire event. You should stick to it as much as possible but know when you need to venture off it to be thorough in the event the witness drops surprises during the deposition. If you adequately prepare for the deposition, your outline should include all the key testimony you need to elicit.

If you find the witness to be evasive with the question before them, do not let them off the hook easily. Ask the same question multiple ways until they state what you need to pin down. This is where the topics on your outline should be used as a checklist more than just a guide. This is your deposition, and you should treat it that way. Lastly, should you venture off the outline to walk down a rabbit hole with the witness, finish that topic point as best as you can and come right back to the outline to make sure you do not miss any points and can conclude in a reasonable amount of time.

HOW TO DEAL WITH AN UNPROFESSIONAL OPPOSING COUNSEL

Simply put, the opposing counsel will attempt to intimidate you during the deposition. To avoid being attacked by opposing counsel, study the permissible objections permitted in your jurisdiction. The opposing counsel may use unprofessional behavior including name calling, sly remarks, and inapplicable objections, and may instruct their client not to answer a question. They typically use these tactics to harass you, get you angry and emotional, and try to throw you off your groove in the deposition. If you have done your homework on the applicable rules and objections, you can win this battle and keep a calm, cool mind. Always ask the opposing counsel to state the basis of their objection so it is recorded in the event the point is crucial to your line of questioning and for a judge to rule.

Remember to keep your cool during the contentious deposition, and your lawyer brain will continue to work. If you get emotional in response to opposing counsel, you will lose your edge and begin thinking the same way your client does. Take a deep breath when you are confronted by opposing counsel and be the lawyer your client needs in the deposition.

CONCLUSION

These tips will be helpful in weighing out whether or not a deposition will be worth the price for your client. Do not shy away from doing depositions simply because you know your client cannot afford it. Depending on how the dress rehearsal goes, the deposition could be used as a settlement tool. The fees for the deposition could save on the far larger costs of going to trial.

10

The Cost-Effective Trial

Trial and preparation for trial are undoubtedly the highest cost to clients. By being pragmatic with your preparation and appearance, you can still reduce the costs.

BEFORE TRIAL

Legal Financing Options

There are times when your client simply does not have the money for trial. It's not fair to either of you with the amount of hard work and preparation you've already put into their case. If you ask for a trial retainer up front, there are legal financing options available to clients and attorneys alike. The client can take a secured and/or an unsecured loan to pay your fees up front. That way the client is able to make lower monthly payments. They will have to use caution with the interest rates. If the matter is a divorce, there are some divorce financing companies that finance legal fees based on their expected monetary award.

Stipulations

Speak with opposing counsel beforehand about the facts you both can agree on. This saves a lot of time on trial. Judges will also appreciate these stipulations taking some of the load off of them. Income for child support purposes is an easy stipulation to come to. Think about how much time you have to spend on introducing pay statements, bank statements, tax returns, health insurance information, childcare costs, etc. Unless there is a legitimate dispute as to one party's income, there's no reason to go through all of the exhibits. It may work to your advantage to stipulate substantive facts when there are certain facts that are unfavorable to your client. It looks like a concession to opposing counsel; but imagine how much worse negative facts will permeate when they are belabored in cross-examination.

Consider carefully how your client would handle responding to addressing the negative facts against them. If you worry that they might lose their temper or perjure themselves, this is a better way out. How will you know if they sink or swim as a witness? That's where the real preparation comes in. To judge the client on their reactions, complete a dress rehearsal of cross-examination of your client and do not pull any punches. A client exposed to the harshness of cross-examination beforehand will be a better witness on the stand.

Preparing Your Client

The more prepared your client is, the less nervous they will be as a witness, and the less nervous you will be about them dropping any bombs in their testimony. Come up with a list of basics that your client should know about testifying. This should apply to anyone, not a particular client. This saves them on fees and you on preparation.

Here are a few tips you can relay to the client during preparation:

1. Speak loudly and clearly.
2. The judge is always watching you: behave even when you are not on the stand. Tell your support group ahead of trial that if they are sitting in the courtroom they cannot be speaking out, talking, or doing anything that might distract the judge or worse, annoy them. It will reflect poorly on you.
3. The courtroom is the judge's temple: do not cut them off, answer the questions you are asked, dress like you would if you were going to church, and do watch your language.
4. Do not tell your attorney anything new when you are on the stand. Your attorney is better able to tell your side of the story when they know what that side is.

5. Write notes, do not try to speak to your attorney at the trial table. Bring a notepad.
6. Do not ramble and stick to the question being asked. Rambling may cause the judge to stop listening, and it will take up more trial time.
7. On cross-examination, stop and think about the question. Explain your answer rather than just saying yes or no.

Pretrial Statement/Order

Filing a pretrial statement/order will give the judge a succinct summary of the case and the issues before the court. Remembering what is in the pretrial statement is easier and more memorable than combing through a voluminous case file. Some jurisdictions require it, but even if they do not, it will still save on trial time. If you file a joint statement with opposing counsel, this is a good opportunity to state any stipulations to the court beforehand.

The court may provide you with the parameters of what is expected from the pretrial statement. Even if it is not required for you to file, it is still helpful to do so. Commonly addressed provisions of a pretrial statement included:

- The contested issues
- Any resolved issues
- A list of witnesses
- A statement of legal authorities
- List of exhibits

Pretrial Motions

Certain pretrial motions could help reduce trial time as well. Motions to strike certain issues, where the other party neglected to follow procedure, may help as well. In the event that the evidence the other side wants to get in your case, these motions are worth a shot.

Discovery motions like Motions in Limine or Motions for Sanctions can help with getting hot-button issues out of the way. Motions in Limine can help keep out evidence that would instead take up considerable trial time when it comes time to object to its entry into evidence. Motions for Sanctions can help narrow the issues as well, depending on the relief allowed by your jurisdiction. Relief to request to help trim down trial time could be as extensive as requesting a complete dismissal of the other side's complaint, requesting that the other side be prohibited from entering in evidence that was requested in discovery or asking for attorney's fees related to the other side's failure to respond to save your client some money for trial costs. The added benefit of these motions is that they let the court know before trial that the other side does not respect the procedure.

DURING TRIAL

The Unnecessary Witnesses

Your client may not understand that they do not need a friend (or several) to randomly attest to their being a good person. If that person has seen them around their kids and can attest to them being a good parent with specificity, that's different. A coworker simply coming in to say the client is a hard worker is not helpful in a custody dispute. Certain witnesses are unnecessarily large consumers of precious trial time. The universal standard is what's in the *best interest of the child*; this is not about the parent. Certainly, character and fitness are a consideration, but make sure a lay witness's testimony relates to the client's fitness as a parent. When the other side brings such a witness, consider whether to even bother to cross-examine them. Not cross-examining them sends an important message to the judge, and that message is that this witness is completely useless. Saving trial time is just a bonus. If the client insists that this witness needs to testify, consider having them write an affidavit to testify, if permissible. This is a win-win: it satisfies the client while still saving the potential wasted trial time.

If it's not your witness, consider consenting to the other party to do an offer of proof (or proffer) instead of putting this witness on. There is a positive side to allowing the other side to proffer with smaller witnesses. If they are willing to do this, you can take opposing counsel outside to hear the proffer first, so you can negotiate what you would agree to. There is also the case of the witness who is there to establish particular negative facts from their personal knowledge against your client. Allowing the proffer of testimony for a witness of this nature can also work to your advantage. There's a chance that this witness could be really good, very detailed, and of course, they will be able to paint a far more accurate and credible story than opposing counsel. Allowing opposing counsel to deliver these facts instead allows you to use your client or other witnesses to attack the proffer with a more detailed account than the proffer.

If it is your witness that is mainly there for their account of narrow observations, consider asking to do an offer of proof as well. First call the witness, determine whether they will be a good witness. Ask yourself, are they likely to ramble on the stand? Are they likely to take a detour from the relevant issues? Would you take them seriously if you were behind the bench? If you feel it would be better to do without this witness, talk to opposing counsel beforehand. This way you do not have to subpoena or bring the witness in for trial. You may want to file something with the court beforehand to acknowledge that you and opposing counsel have agreed to allow an offer of proof, so the judge does not demand that the witness be present.

Keep Opening/Closing Concise, and Highlight Theme Throughout

Openings and closings are exciting. They are where a lawyer can make arguments eloquently to string the evidence together and tell the story that testimony alone cannot. The laws of primary and recency are in our favor. It is a common misconception that openings and closings are supposed to be long-winded like those in televised criminal trials. But (unless you're in Texas) you're not speaking to a jury. You're speaking to a judge, who is in charge of many other staff members in the courtroom and who expects to be able to go to lunch or go home at the end of the day. Judges who go the distance and stay after hours are far and few. Keep your openings and closings concise. In your opening, establish a theme for your case and address the points that will really grab the judge's attention. If there is abuse or neglect by the other party, start with that. It is helpful to repeat what you are requesting at both the opening and closing. Use your client's full name and introduce them to the judge in the opening statement. This will humanize them even more to a judge who sees your client as a total stranger.

Use the theme in your opening to summarize your case in your closing as well. For example, "Mother puts her self-interest before the child's, whereas father puts the child first." When you address the theme in the opening, highlight the most pertinent facts from the evidence that will reflect this, such as mother withheld the child after the separation because she was mad, mother wants primary custody for higher child support, mother makes unilateral decisions without consulting father, mother argues with and disparages father in front of the children, etc. Then contrast these with the father's positive traits such as willingness to co-parent, not withholding the child, communicating respectfully, etc. Then home in on these points through your evidence. Finish your opening statement with stating exactly what you're wanting from the court. Be as specific as possible because judges typically write this down as you're talking. An example would be, "Today we are asking this honorable court to modify legal and physical custody from the Mother to the Father for the above stated reasons. We are further asking that child support be set at an amount no less than $800 per month and including an order that the minor children shall not be around the Mother's new boyfriend, Joseph Smith, unsupervised at any time." Judges like clarity and knowing exactly why you're in their courtroom.

In closing, go over the law that the judge needs to consider and highlight the testimony that was in your favor, especially when it comes from the other side. Keep in mind that by the time of closing, the judge may have already rendered their decision.

Evidence

Self-authenticating exhibits are very helpful. They will save time at trial so that you do not have to deal with objections from opposing counsel and risk the objection eventually being sustained. Try to agree to the admission of exhibits with opposing counsel. That will save time on at least some objections.

Supplement Discovery

More than a month prior to trial, discuss with your client what evidence you may still need. Put the client to work again to update the documents already provided since your discovery responses were provided. Supplementing financial documents beforehand may lead to you reaching an agreement on financial issues or stipulations on income with opposing counsel.

Objections

Objections will disrupt your flow in examination and could distract you, the witness, or the judge from crucial information. Further, consider whether an objection is proper. Just because something may be hearsay, you don't want to be viewed as "that lawyer." The idea is not to sit in your trial seat as if a thumbtack is under your backside. If it is harmless, let the story be told. You may pick up an opportunity to hammer the other side's witness from your allowing them to talk. You would have missed this, had you stifled the dialogue.

SETTLEMENT DURING TRIAL

Most lawyers know when they are fighting a losing battle, especially those who are familiar with the judge trying their case. It's not worth it to spend time in trial when you and even your client know what's coming. Try and talk to the judge in chambers about the case; see if they have any suggestions for settlement. If you don't reach a settlement based on the judge's recommendation, frequently that judge ends up ruling the exact way they suggested. Judges typically do not hesitate to provide their concerns and thoughts prior to a trial after hearing a quick summary from each side. After you hear the concerns, you can take this information back to the client and let them know what the judge thinks. The client then may have the "reality check" necessary to think logically and clearly on how to settle the case.

Another effective method is having the judge put the fear in the client's mind of what a gamble going to trial is. When you have a good chance at success, make sure to look to see whether the other party has met their burden under the law. This could get the case dismissed during trial in the form of a directed verdict and/or motion for summary judgment. In domestic violence hearings, some acts of abuse simply don't apply between people who are married or have children together. For instance, in Maryland acts like stalking or harassment may not apply for a protective order, even though these acts may be necessary to further the best interests of the child. If you represent the respondent, make a motion to dismiss at the end of the petitioner's case. There's no need for you to waste time putting forth a defense when the petitioner's case can just as easily be dismissed.

Use of Demonstrative Exhibits

There are many things that can be summed up in a demonstrative exhibit. They are specifically helpful for financial records and visit logs. It will take the time to get this information into evidence, but if your jurisdiction allows for the admission of demonstrative exhibits with advance notice to opposing counsel, do so. A demonstrative exhibit helps the judge condense all of the information that you are introducing. It goes a long way; for example, if you want to summarize cash withdrawals from a bank report, create a demonstrative exhibit showing the dates and amounts of withdrawals, rather than having to introduce hundreds of bank statements. Whether we acknowledge it or not, judges are human. You don't know what kind of learner they are. These exhibits can still be helpful to you to condense the case, regardless of whether the judge accepts it.

In cases where the client is being denied access, a full list of visits, contacts, and attempts made to have visitation has been quite helpful. This is the kind of exhibit where the client has to do the work. Get your client to keep a log from the onset of the case. They will save time on your work in creating the document; it is far quicker than you having to go through all of your notes from all of the conversations you have had with your clients. Another idea would be to print a blank calendar available in a quick internet search and have them document when your client received the minor children. It will show, in a clear format, how your client was denied visits with the children.

Summarizing expenses of the other party is a great way to use demonstrative exhibits. In child support cases, play up bank records and credit card statements of the opposing party. It certainly helps to show the disposable income of the opposing party. It can also work against their character. When there's a history of drinking problems, go through all of the charges to liquor stores. If the other party is claiming to be impoverished, summarize the luxury or unnecessary expenses from their bank statements. If they are not actually spending time with the child during their access, look for bar charges, out-of-state charges, or any other adult activities where the kids are obviously not, or should not, be with them. If the other party is trying to win the child over with gifts, highlight the differences in toy and entertainment expenses before and after trial. If the other party is self-employed, look through the expenses that are in their business accounts but are obviously for leisure. This is helpful when the other party has filed a financial statement misrepresenting their actual income. Microsoft Excel spreadsheets can easily show the total sum of the opposing party's questionable expenses. Color coding, highlighting, bolding, and underlining the total grabs more attention than voluminous or wordy documents.

POST JUDGMENT

There's no real winning in family law. Even if you feel you won, your client may be hung up on what they didn't win on a small trivial issue. Other times the judge leaves out smaller aspects in their orders, like holidays and phone calls. Try to negotiate these after the fact with opposing counsel, to see if you can get what your client wants. Yes, negotiation will cost your client money, but it is cheaper than them having to file an appeal. It also possibly prevents future modifications.

Another trick to avoiding an appeal is to file a revisory motions to help with fixing minor issues and even possibly major issues, depending on the audience. A motion to reconsider or a motion to alter or amend judgement may help get your client the win on smaller issues after the trial. This is a far better alternative to an appeal in instances when your client takes issue with the specifics or lack thereof in the judgment. For example, if the judge leaves the details of where custody exchanges shall occur, you can file a post-judgment motion to get what your client wants in that instance.

If there's nowhere else to go but an appeal, see what cost-effective options your jurisdiction may have. In Maryland, there is an appeal option to file for an in banc review. This prohibits an appeal to the higher court but allows for an appeal to a panel of new judges within the trial court. Instead of a heavy brief, this option requires a simple memorandum. An appellate brief and record are going to be far more costly to the client. Get a list of low bono appeals resources, law school appeals clinics, or pro bono services that would work for an appeal.

CONCLUSION

The tips in this chapter help make the actual trial as affordable as possible. Using them should allow the client's story to be told persuasively and effectively at a custody trial, minimize damage from the other side, and allowing the client to be the best prepared narrator of their own story.

11

Litigating Child Custody in a Pandemic

The COVID-19 pandemic has undoubtedly changed court proceedings and the practice of law. Advocating for clients in a courtroom full of people went from to face-to-face to a video screen. Tendering exhibits printed in triplicate is now emailing the court a Zip file containing all exhibits at once. Given this new reality, this chapter is absolutely necessary for concluding the book. The technology and overall advocacy tips in this chapter can make the remote courtroom a little easier to manage.

NECESSARY PANDEMIC TECHNOLOGY

Given that most trials nowadays are using video conferencing software, try to become an expert on the technology your jurisdiction uses. Study the "how to" guides on the software websites. The customer service of the software is very helpful, in our experience, should the questions you may have not be listed. If the court provides you with login instructions beforehand, make sure to test out the technology. Do the same with your client, and make sure they have the software or application downloaded to avoid technological difficulties. If the court will allow it, it may be better for evidentiary hearings to have your client be present with you. The court can then see the exhibits being authenticated.

Backup Internet Access

For video trials, you are likely sitting at your home office connected to the internet via Wi-Fi. Do not fall into a false sense of security with your home network. If your internet decides to short out on the day of trial, your trial could be ruined. To resolve this issue, do video trials on a device that is connected to a data plan, or use a personal hotspot. If these options are not available, consider plugging the computer directly into the router to avoid spotty Wi-Fi at home. A Wi-Fi booster may also be a good investment should you be working from home for the foreseeable future. This affordable solution can distribute the Wi-Fi signal evenly throughout your home if your standard router is not living up to expectations.

Webcams

The presentation of both counsel and clients should not change from the way it was in person. Do not settle for a mediocre webcam or cell phone camera. Go for a high-definition (HD) camera for court appearances. These tend to avoid the "whitewashed" look for the court. Cameras are like televisions: the higher the resolution, the better the quality of your appearance. Opt for 1080p or 4K for the resolution. A 1080p-resolution webcam can be mounted to the top of the computer monitor. The webcam uses a USB port and is plug-and-play–ready for your usage. These particular cameras are available online and typically cost under $50.

Microphone and Audio

As with webcams, relying upon the preinstalled microphone on your laptop or desktop may not be your best option. Consider a higher-quality microphone, for example, the Blue Snowball USB Microphone by YETI. The sound quality for speaking to the court goes unmatched.

Another great investment is a pair of high-quality headphones. Oftentimes, the quality of computer speakers is only average. If you are in a financial position to purchase it, try a pair of noise-cancelling headphones. The sound quality is typically better than standard headphones. The noise-cancelling feature is also great for drowning out the sounds of other family members working at home, should you need the peace and quiet.

Invest in a High-Quality Home Office Chair

Since you are going to spend most of your work from home time sitting down, do not settle for the dining room chairs. They do not serve your spine very well, causing you to stand up more frequently, dampening your productivity. Find a chair that suits your body type and taste. Simulating the office environment at home will not only help you keep your focus; it also appears far more professional during remote hearings and meeting.

ETIQUETTE FOR VIDEO TRIALS

Now that you have the technology to make you appear your best on a video trial, it is important to discuss the etiquette to govern your video trial. The first should be to create a clean, distraction-free environment to maximize your focus. Only have out the documents needed for your trial at hand. Put the other documents for your firm away. It is also recommended that you should turn off all other noise-making software and programs on your computer. Lawyers whose phones are repeatedly going off while they are conducting a video trial appear unprofessional and distracted. You should silence not only your cell phone notifications but also your landline if you have one in your home office and/or real office. Further, if you are working from home with children and/or even your spouse present, you should design a sign for your home office door with a COURT IN SESSION notice. This also works for your real office door to alert staff and other attorneys not to enter. You may have heard of lawyers wearing only the top portion of a suit and just boxer briefs below the waist. Do not be that lawyer. After the trial is over, take the tie off and unbutton the top button to feel comfortable. Remember your client is paying you for this trial with or without in-person trial. Be the attorney they need and hired.

HOW TO MAKE YOUR EXHIBITS READY FOR TRIAL

If you don't already have those small rectangular exhibit stickers, now is a good time to get them. It's important to label your exhibits prior to delivering or e-filing them. It avoids confusion, saves the clerk time, and will make the virtual presentation to the witness far easier. You can always call them out of order and acknowledge it on the record if the court will allow you to do so. If you don't already know, ask the court early on what labels they would prefer. For example, the court may prefer that plaintiff's exhibits be numbered exhibits that the defendant's be lettered.

Call the court well in advance to see how they would prefer you provide the exhibits. Even some courts with e-filing will still prefer you to hand-deliver them. Typically, you will be emailed the login information. Use the clerk who sent the email as a point of contact. If they want the exhibits dropped off, remember to do so a few days in advance. Dropping them off yourself or having them couriered may be the best way to ensure they get there in time. For further assurances, email the exhibits to the clerk and opposing counsel as well. This practice is a little bit tricky, because opposing counsel will know what exhibits you intend to use and when in trial you intend to use it, and from there they can infer what witnesses are being called. However, I try not to disclose impeachment or rebuttal evidence at this time, especially if it is audio or video. If it is audio or video, you can simply play the audio and share the screen for video. Make sure to mail the file on a thumb drive to the court thereafter. For written statements, rather than try and enter in the actual document, just read from the document in cross-examination. For example, "Didn't you say at the August 4th hearing that you 'would never pay him a dime in child support because frankly he didn't deserve it'?"

WARNINGS OF SHORTCOMINGS OF VIDEO TRIALS

This chapter would be incomplete without pointing out the unforeseen flaws of video trials. Aside from the main flaws including spotty internet, delays in dialogue between attorney and a party, and stating objections without speaking over someone, there are others. These flaws include potential tainting of testimony by a lawyer texting his client on what to say during testimony and/or someone in the same room as the client coaching him/her.

Further, video trials lead to difficulty authenticating documents compared to in-person trials. Sharing your computer screen for the video trial is the best option for showing a document to the witness, but this option is difficult to navigate, and skimming pages contained in a document packet is not as smooth on the screen as submitting the paper copy in an in-person hearing.

Lastly, because this book is centered towards modest-means clients, technology itself may be problematic. The author represents clients in rural areas where high-speed internet is not always available. Thankfully, most clients nowadays have smartphones and have decent cell phone coverage at their home. Also consider the client's age and technology knowledge: there are many clients who do not like and/or do not use advanced technology. If the client needs to use the camera on their phone, prepare them remotely and teach them how to position their camera. The client should be looking directly at the camera just as they would with a computer, which may require some props to get the phone on that level. Make it clear to them that they need to be in a room alone with no background distractions. Not in their car, not at work, and not outside. Also make sure they would dress just as they would if the case were conducted in person. Planning ahead here will help some but will not solve all issues with these clients. If your court allows the client to sit on the video trial next to their lawyer, you can be the technology expert for your client and make the video trial as smooth as possible.

CONCLUSION

The technology and ideas in this chapter will have you appearing at your best in the virtual courtroom. Following this advice will allow you to be heard clearly, look your best on video, and present your case as professionally as you would in person under the circumstances.

12
Final Points

Clients do not always have the money to get the representation they deserve. The tips and ideas in this book are intended to give you new avenues to do your job effectively regardless of limiting financial circumstances.

Attorneys who are hired by modest-means clients know to zealously advocate for them by fully using the resources available. The ideas in this book should be used as a roadmap to getting the evidence and information required for your case. It is important to remember that whatever evidence you seek out and find using our ideas must be tied back to the child in the custody litigation. It is a common argument that a parent is unfit to parent because of their poor choices or lack of morals. Remember that being a bad person does not equate to being a bad parent. Tie the information to how the opposing party actually parents the child.

Your fees will have a significant impact on your relationship with the client. When you are conscious of the client's financial constraints, they will trust that you are in this field to help and advocate for them, not bleed them dry. Their faith in you is what will make or break the attorney–client relationship.

Most of us went to law school to help people. Helping people should not be defined by how affluent your clients are. With a large number of people representing themselves in family law courts throughout the United

States, there is plenty of work for practitioners to market affordable services to lower-income individuals. The ideas in this book will get the information you need at a fraction of the cost (if not free) to achieve the goals of both the attorney and the client: the attorney has a paying client who requires less manual labor; the client hires an attorney who can help them navigate the complicated family law journey without being driven to bankruptcy. Ultimately, the costs of litigation for lower-income clients will limit the resources of the children they hired you to fight for.

Appendix

1. Sample Engagement Letter for Contested Child Custody Matter
2. Commonly Requested Documents List in Child Custody Litigation
3. Child Custody Case Intake Form
4. Subpoena for Production of Documents
5. Child Custody Interrogatories
6. Request for Production of Documents for Child Custody Cases

Sample Engagement Letter for Contested Child Custody Matter

1. Introduction

This letter constitutes our agreement for representing you in a child custody case against Deanna Defendant. Please read it carefully and call me if you have any questions about it. Please discuss this engagement letter with your regular family or business lawyer if you like.

If you find this agreement acceptable, please sign on the last page of the original of this letter, initial pages 1 through 4 in the lower left-hand corner and return it to us. You may keep the copy of this Agreement marked "Copy." The receipt of the signed original by our office, along with your advance flat fee non-refundable payment of $__________for fees and costs, will initiate our representation of you.

2. Counseling

If you are not presently in counseling, our office recommends that you consider it. Oftentimes, the length and expense of the case is usually affected by the intensity of the parties' feelings towards each other and general emotions. During a family law matter many people experience emotions that are difficult to handle without professional help. We find that the money invested in psychological help is well spent because the client is better able to cope with the stress of the case. Counseling often results in reduced attorneys' fees.

3. Costs

In addition to the attorney rates described above, you also will pay any out-of-pocket costs incurred in your case. Typical costs incurred include but are not limited to: photocopies, postage, word processing, long-distance telephone calls and faxes, legal research time, process servers, court filing fees, court reporters, witness fees, out-of-town travel, experts, and investigators. We will not hire experts or investigators unless you agree that they should be hired and that you will pay directly for their services.

4. Progress of Your Case

We shall keep you well informed as to the progress of your case. We require all clients to check their email daily to ensure he/she misses no communication from our office. We shall send you copies of all papers coming in and going out of our offices, including correspondence, pleadings, and other court documents via email and/or the client's "portal" through CLIO. If no one is available when you telephone, your call shall be returned promptly provided you leave a detailed message on our voicemail box. The file and its progress are open to your inspection at any reasonable time and request.

5. Payment of Legal Fees by Opposing Party

Sometimes in child custody litigation, the Court may order one party to pay the other party's legal fees and costs. In appropriate circumstances, we will ask the Court to order the other party to pay your fees and costs. In any event, you are responsible for the amount due to us from you.

Should the other party pay fees ordered by the Court, you shall be reimbursed any amounts over your total bill. In child custody cases, attorney fees are not awarded to the "prevailing party," but are awarded, if at all, as the Court deems just and proper under the circumstances. This is more likely to happen when one party has substantially more income and/or causes the other party to incur fees and costs by his or her conduct during the litigation.

In addition, if you are the party with more income and assets, or if you cause the other party to incur fees and costs by your conduct, the Court may order you to pay all or a portion of the opposing party's fees.

6. Client Duties

You, as the client, agree to tell us the truth, to keep us advised of your address, email address, and telephone number, to cooperate in the preparation and trial of your case, to appear on reasonable notice for Court appearances and depositions, to pay our bills on time, and to comply with all reasonable requests made of you in connection with the preparation and presentation of this matter including discovery.

You agree not to settle or compromise the claims without discussing the matter with us, and we agree not to settle or compromise your claims without your informed consent. You agree to call for an appointment so that we can be prepared to discuss your case with you. "Drop-in visits" seldom result in as much value to a client as do scheduled appointments as we may not be in the office the day you stop by. You can help us provide the best service for the least cost with your cooperation.

7. No Guarantees of Outcome

You acknowledge and understand that our office has made no guarantees regarding the outcome of your case or about issues that may be decided by the Court. Statements that we make regarding the likely outcome, or the range of possible outcomes are only our opinions based upon our knowledge and experience—and are not guarantees of results.

8. Scope of Representation

The provisions of this agreement shall apply only to the matter referenced above and, unless otherwise specifically provided, our representation of you shall be for trial court proceedings only. If appellate proceedings are necessary or if you want to institute appellate proceedings, additional fees and advance payment arrangements must be made. If we continue to represent you after final judgment or after our initial undertaking is completed, all of these provisions shall apply and we shall each be bound by these terms, unless we have a written agreement to the contrary.

Further, should you wish to engage with us in another legal matter (criminal, estate planning, etc.), said representation shall only be initiated upon a new engagement letter and after any discussed fees are paid.

9. Discharge and Withdrawal

You have a right to discharge me as your attorney at any time; however, in such event you agree that I shall be entitled to the payment of all my fees described in paragraph 1 above plus any costs advanced by me pursuant to paragraph 3 above.

I have a right to withdraw as your attorney, if you misrepresent or fail to disclose any material fact to us; if you fail to follow our reasonable advice; you do not maintain consistent contact; if you fail to make payments as required by this agreement; or if you demand that we do something unlawful or unethical.

10. Confidentiality
Communications with us concerning your case are generally confidential and are protected from disclosure under attorney-client privilege rules. This privilege is not absolute, and I may be required to reveal information if necessary to prevent a crime or fraud upon the Court. Your privilege of confidentiality can also be lost if you discuss our communications with other persons outside of our office. If the Court is asked to decide the issue of attorneys' fees in this case, this agreement may be disclosed to the Court. If, at any time, you have questions about confidentiality, please call me to discuss it.

11. Closing
I look forward to working with you on this case. We welcome and encourage your input and suggestions. Please do not hesitate to contact me if you have any questions and/or concerns.

Sincerely,

____
Attorney

Accepted and agreed this ____________.

____
Paul Plaintiff-Client

Commonly Requested Documents List in Child Custody Litigation

Please be proactive and retrieve these documents early to avoid missing discovery deadlines. This list further assists your attorney in advocating for your child custody case:

1. Prior Court Orders, if any, between you and the other parent.
2. Pay Statements for your employment for at least the past one year.
3. Tax Returns (State & Federal) for the past five years.
4. Banking Statements of all of the accounts you have access to for, at least, the past one year.
5. Credit Card Statements from the past two years minimum.
6. Any documentation to prove you have paid and/or received child support payments (It may be banking statements, cancelled checks, money orders, etc.)
7. Educational Records relating to the child in this matter for the past two years minimum.
8. Any Medical records relating to the child(ren)'s current diagnosis, if any.
9. Dental records of the minor child.
10. Documents relating to the minor child's therapist treating the child(ren).
11. Any documentation relating to the child(ren)'s extracurricular activities.
12. Any lease agreements and/or mortgage statements relating to your current residence.
13. Any prior criminal history you and/or the other parent was accused of (regardless of conviction).
14. Copies of any health insurance in which the minor children are covered. Provide both the cards and any explanation of benefits under said coverage. Repeat this for any dental, life, and vision insurance for the minor child(ren).
15. Your mandatory financial disclosure affidavit.
16. A copy of any passports in your possession for the minor children.
17. Telephone records for the past two years.
18. Any calendars you maintained as it relates to visitation with the other parent and the minor child(ren).
19. Any evidence of domestic violence between you and the other parent.
20. Any documents relating to any substance abuse by either you or the other parent.
21. Text communication records between you and the other parent. Provide any other format of communication between you and the other parent (e.g., Facebook, Twitter, Snapchat, etc.).

Child Custody Case Intake Form

____
First Name Last Name Middle Initial

Mailing Address: _______________________________.

____

Street number and name ___________________________

____
City State Zip Code

How long have you resided at this address?:______________

Home Phone: ______________

Work Phone: ______________

Cell Phone: ______________

Physical Address (if different): ___________________

____

Street number and name ___________________________

____
City State Zip Code

Email Address: ______________

Does the other parent have access to this email address? Y N ________

Employer (Name and Address): ______________________

Social Security Number: ___________________

Date of Birth: ___________________

Who may we contact if we cannot get in contact with you?

____
First Name Middle Last Name Phone Number

Other Parent's Information:

____
First Name Last Name Middle Initial

Mailing address: ____

____

Street number and name ____

____

City State Zip Code

How long has he/she resided at this address?: ______________

Home Phone: ______________

Work Phone: ______________

Cell Phone: ______________

Email Address: ______________

Employer (Name and Address): ____________________________

Social Security Number (if known):

Date of Birth:

Briefly State the Reason for Today's Consultation:

CHILD(REN)'S INFORMATION:

How many children are at issue in this case?

Name: ______________ DOB: _____ SSN: ______________ M F

Name: ______________ DOB: _____ SSN: ______________ M F

Name: ______________ DOB: _____ SSN: ______________ M F

Where is/are the child(ren) currently residing? ______________

List all addresses where your child(ren) have lived for the past five years. Include the address, the known dates of living at this residence, and with whom the child(ren) lived?

Name & Address of the Child(ren)'s School: ______________

What grade is/are the child/children currently in?

What kind of grades are the child(ren) receiving at this time?

Please describe any educational issues you may have about the child(ren).

Name & Address/Contact Information for Child Care Provider(s):

Child(ren)'s Current Extracurricular Activities:

How long have they been involved in these activities?

Any known activities for the children from the past?

Who paid for said activities?

OTHER INFORMATION:

Were you ever married to the opposing party?

If yes, Date of the Marriage? ____________

Date of Separation? __________________

Date of Divorce Granted? ____________________

Is there a current custody order in place? Y N

If yes, What County granted the order/divorce? ____________________

If yes, Which Judge granted the order/divorce? ____________________

Did you bring a copy of the Order Y N

If not, please briefly describe what the order states as you understand it regarding custody: ____________________

If there has not been a custody order:

Has paternity been established? Y N

When was paternity established? ____________

Is there an active child support order? Y N

Is child support currently being paid? Y N

By Whom? ______________

How much each month? ______________

Is the opposing party currently behind in child support? Y N

By how much? $___________

Who carries medical/dental insurance on the child(ren)? ______________

Monthly expense? $_____________

Are there childcare expenses? Y N

If so, how much? _________________

Who pays? ________________

Financial Information:

Gross monthly wages for the Father: $__________ __________

Gross monthly wages for the Mother: $__________ __________

Do you want the opposing party to have joint legal custody? Y N _____

If No, State why:

Do you want the opposing party to have visitation? Y N _____

If no, are you comfortable with the other parent having supervised visitation? If supervised visitations are requested, please state your reasons:

Please state the parenting time arrangement/goals you would like to see come out of this matter. Please list any particular holidays or events that you find of significant importance to be in a Parenting Plan by the Court:

<u>Additional Child(ren) Information:</u>

Please list your children's present:

Religion: ______________________

Church the child attends (Name & Address):

Child's Current Pediatrician (Name & Address):

Child's Current Dentist (Name & Address):

Child's Current Therapist (Name & Address):

Child Recreational Activities Location (Name & Address/Contact Info.):

Subpoena for Production of Documents

STATE OF GEORGIA ________________COUNTY
TO: _______County Department of Family and Children's Services
123 Main Street ANYTOWN, ST ZIP

You are hereby commanded, that laying all other business aside, you shall be and appear at the Superior Court before the presiding judge in the _______ County Courthouse, TOWN, Georgia to be held on March ____, 202__ at ________A.M./P.M. to be sworn as a witness for the Defendant in the case of *Plaintiff v. Defendant*, Civil Action Number: _________.

The following are hereby subpoenaed:

All records currently in the possession of the ________County Department of Family & Children's Services relating to FIRST PARENT and/or SECOND PARENT to include all documents, audio recordings, videos, photographs, and the names of any witnesses. Such records must be present on or before March ______, 2021 at ___________A.M./P.M. for in camera inspection to the Honorable Judge ____________ pursuant to amended O.C.G.A. § 49-5-40.

You are required to attend from day to day and from time to time until the matter is disposed of.

HEREIN FAIL NOT, under penalty of law by authority of the Honorable _____________, Judge of said Court this _____day of ____________, 2021.

Any questions, please contact:

Samuel E. Thomas
PO Box 80004
Athens, Georgia 30605
706-555-1234

Hon. CLERK NAME
Clerk of Superior Court
_______County, Georgia
706-555-4567

____
Subpoena issued by Attorney of Record for the Plaintiff/Defendant

RETURN OF SERVICE

I served the within witness __________County Department of Family & Children's Services with this subpoena on MONTH _____, 2021 at ____a.m./p.m. by: ___ to him/her in person.

Served by: ______________________________________
Name and Title

IN THE SUPERIOR COURT OF ___________COUNTY
STATE OF GEORGIA

PAUL PLAINTIFF, *

Plaintiff *

v.

* Civil Action #

DEANNA DEFENDANT, *

Defendant *

-MOTION SEEKING RECORDS AND REQUESTING IN CAMERA INSPECTION-

COMES NOW, Paul Plaintiff, Plaintiff, by and through his counsel of record, and hereby moves this Court to issue an order making records relating to Deanna Defendant, available to the parties' counsel in the above-styled action and shows this Honorable Court as follows:

1.

Counsel for Defendant has contemporaneously prepared subpoenas for service on The Department of Family and Children's Services of ________County. A true and accurate copy of the subpoena is attached hereto as "Exhibit-A."

2.

Georgia law was amended by the legislature in 2016, effectively changing the process whereby such records may be requested. *(O.C.G.A. §49-5-40; 49-5-41) O.C.G.A. § 49-5-41(11)* provides that:

A court, by subpoena that is filed contemporaneously with a motion seeking records and requesting an in-camera inspection of such records, may make such records available to a party seeking such records when:

A. Such motion is filed;
B. Such motion is served;
    a. On all parties to the action;
    b. On the department or other entity that has possession of such records, as applicable; and
    c. In matters other than a dependency proceeding or a civil proceeding wherein there is no related pending criminal investigation or prosecution of criminal or unlawful activity, on the prosecuting attorney, as applicable; and
C. After an in-camera inspection of such records, the court finds that access to such records appears reasonably calculated to lead to the discovery of admissible evidence.

3.

Plaintiff believes that access to the records relating to the allegations now in the custody and control of these agencies is reasonably calculated to lead to the discovery of admissible evidence.

4.

Plaintiff believes these records to be relevant and of significant importance to the issues in the above-styled action, as such records contain prior incidents against Defendant.

WHEREFORE, the Plaintiff respectfully requests that:

a) The Court review the records from ______County Department of Family and Children Services, find that access to such records is likely to lead to the discovery of admissible and relevant evidence, and issue a protective order as required by *O.C.G.A § 49-5-41(g)(3)* to ensure the confidentiality of such records, upon penalty of contempt.

Submitted this _____ day of ___________, 2021.

____
Attorney NAME, Esq.
State Bar No.
Attorney for Plaintiff/Defendant

Law Office of ___________
PO Box NUMBER
CITY, STATE ZIP
706-555-1234|
Fax: 706-555-4567
email@domain.com

Child Custody Interrogatories

If you contend that your spouse is unfit to have custody of the children, state the facts upon which your contention is based and identify all persons having personal knowledge of these facts. If your contention is based on the use of controlled dangerous substances or the abuse of alcohol on specific occasions, identify the substance used, the other persons present at the time of the use, and the date, time, and place of the use. If your contention is based on the repeated use of controlled dangerous substances or the repeated abuse of alcohol, identify the substance and all persons with personal knowledge of the repeated use or abuse.[1]

If you have sought or received treatment or therapy at any time during the past 10 years for any physical, mental, or emotional condition, including drug addiction or alcoholism, describe the condition and the treatment or therapy provided, state the date or dates of treatment or therapy, and identify all persons providing treatment or therapy. *Id.*

If you contend that placing the children in your sole, shared, or joint custody will be in their best interest, specify the facts and circumstances upon which you rely. *Id.*

Describe the childcare plan you intend to follow when the children are with you. Include in your answer a description of the place where the children will reside, specifying the number of bedrooms, bathrooms, and other rooms, the distance to the school which the children will attend, and the identity of all other persons who will be residing in that household. Identify all persons who will care for the children in your absence, state the hours during which they will care for the children, and the location where the care will be provided. *Id.*

List each communication that the other parent has made with you to see the children since your separation. Include in your answer, the date, time, request, and whether or not the request was granted. For each instance in which you denied a request to see the children, please state your reason for the denial.

Describe in detail the custody/access schedule(s) that you and the other parent have followed since your separation through the present. Include in your Answer the child's primary residence, the frequency, days, and times of visitation with each parent, the number of overnights with each parent in a given time period, the holiday/vacation/summer schedule that you and the other parent followed and how you and the other parent came to follow said custody/access schedule. If you and the other parent followed more than one custody/access schedule, so state and include in your Answer the details of each custody/access schedule, the dates on which each particular custody/access schedule was followed by you and the other parent and the reason(s) for the change(s) in the custody/access schedule.

Describe in detail each party's involvement in the child's life, management of health/medical issues, discipline, school choices, religious upbringing, and any

[1] West's Annotated Code of Maryland, Maryland Rules, Title 2. Civil Procedure—Circuit Court Form Interrogatories (Refs & Annos), Form No. 5-DOMESTIC RELATIONS INTERROGATORIES.

other major issues impacting the child, from the date of her birth to the present. Include in your Answer what efforts were made by each party to be involved in each aspect of the child's life, approximately when each party made such efforts, what efforts you made to include the other parent in these aspects of the child's life, and what efforts you have made to include the other parent in these aspects of the child's life.

State with specificity what you believe to be an appropriate access schedule for the other parent and the minor child, including vacations and holidays, and why you have such belief, including in your Answer all facts to support such belief. If you believe the other parent's access should be supervised, state the names, addresses, and contact information, for any persons or supervised visitation programs that you believe should supervise the visitation.

Describe your past communications with the other parent regarding major decisions involving the child including, but not limited to, the method of communication, and the substance of the communication. For any disagreements that have arisen during or as a result of the communications note each party's position and the final resolution.

Describe in detail, including specifically approximate dates and/or events, any complaints you have as to the care and treatment which the other parent has provided the minor child during her lifetime, including the name, address, and telephone number of each person with personal knowledge thereof. This includes, but is not limited to, any incidents in which you believe the other parent posed a risk of harm to the minor child, and/or caused you concern for the safety of the minor child.

Request for Production of Documents for Child Custody Cases

I herewith serve upon you the following Request for Production of Documents under the provisions of §34 of the Georgia Civil Practice Act (*O.C.G.A. S 9-11-34*). You are requested to produce the documents herein set forth at the Law Office of ____________, ADDRESS, CITY, Georgia ZIP, on or before the 30th day after service of this request upon you, where facilities are available for proper copying.

Pursuant to *O.C.G.A. § 24-13-27*, you are hereby notified to produce in the courtroom of the presiding Judge, at any temporary hearing or hearing upon motion, deposition, trial, or any other proceeding in the above-styled case, to term from day to day until term is concluded the following books, writings, documents or other tangible objects in the custody or control of Defendant, to wit:

-INSTRUCTIONS-

I. In the event that any document requested is withheld on the basis of a claim of privilege, that document shall be identified by setting forth the following information:

1. The name of the author of the document;
2. The date of the document;
3. The name of each person or persons (other than stenographic or clerical assistant) participating in the preparation of the document;
4. The date on which the document was received by those having possession of the document;
5. The name and address of each person, if any, to whom the contents of the documents have heretofore been communicated by copy, exhibition, reading, or substantial summarization;
6. A brief description of the nature of the subject matter of the document;
7. The statute, rule, or decision that is claimed to give rise to the privilege;
8. The present custodian and location of the document;
9. Attachments to the document;
10. The number of pages, attachments, or appendices comprising the document;
11. Whether the document is handwritten, typewritten, or otherwise prepared; and
12. The number of the request to which the document is responsive.

II. If, for reasons other than a claim of privilege, you refuse to produce any documents described herein, please state the grounds upon which the refusal is based with sufficient specificity to permit a determination of the propriety of such refusal.

III. As used herein, the term "document" shall mean the original, and if not available, any copy of the original, of writings of every kind, including but not limited to every correspondence, drawings, changes to such drawings, sketches, books, records, logs, reports, memoranda, abstracts, advertisements, agreements, appointment records, audio recordings, whether transcribed or not, balance sheets, bills, bills of lading, blanks, books of account, cablegrams, certificates, charters, communications, charts, checks, compilations from which information can be obtained or translated through detection devices, papers, transcriptions or summaries of conversations, delivery records, diaries, drafts, drafts of documents, electronic or mechanical recordation in whatever medium, discs, plans and specifications, graphs, tapes, slides, cards, wires, computer programs, computer printouts, entries, estimates, expense records, field notes, films, financial analyses, financial statements, forms, handbooks, telegrams, income statements, indices, instruments, intra-office and inter-office communications, invoices, itemizations, journals, letters, licenses, manuals, maps, meeting reports, minutes, notes, order forms, orders, opinions, payroll records, permits, photocopies, photographs, planographs, press releases, prospectuses, publications, receipts, recordings, records, records of account, reports, requisitions, resolutions, statement, statistical records, studies, summaries, system analyses, time records, training manuals, evaluations, warehouse receipts, wire transfers, records of wire transfers and any other electronic or mechanical records or transcripts of any other device or instrument from which information can be perceived, or which is used to memorialize human thought, speech, or action in the possession, custody, or control of the party to whom this pleading is directed wherever located, including all premises and residences owned by or used by said party, and all the residences and premises owned or used by any of said party's employees, servants, or representatives. The term "document" shall also include copies containing information in addition to that contained in or on the original and all the attachments, appendices, enclosures, or documents referred to in any documents produced pursuant to this request. If any tape, disc, card, wire, or other electronic or mechanical recording or transcript or any computer program is produced, the party to whom this pleading is directed or other provider of the document or item shall also produce such documents or devices as are necessary for the decoding, playing back, printing, and/or interpretation thereof, and any other documents or devices which are necessary to convert such information into a useful and usable format.

IV. The terms "plaintiff" and "defendant" when used herein includes the person listed as such above, any agents, servants, representatives, or any other person or persons acting for or purportedly acting on such person's behalf.

V. "Relating to" or "which supports" shall mean consisting of, referring to, reflecting, pertaining to, or in any way logically or factually connected with the matter discussed. A document "relating to" or "which supports" a given subject, claim or defense, is any document identifying, showing, referring to, dealing with, evidencing, commenting upon, having as a subject, describing, summarizing, analyzing, explaining, detailing, outlining, defining, interpreting, or pertaining to that subject, including without limitation documents referring to the presentation of other documents.

-REQUESTS-

1. COMPENSATION AND INCOME INFORMATION
   a. Regarding your income sources, please provide all pay stubs, statements of income/earnings, W-2 forms, 1099 forms, K-1 forms, and any other compensation documents given to you by your employer and/or any other person, business, partnership, corporation, or other entity/institution showing your taxable income, tax-free income and other compensation of any kind you have received or are entitled to receive from any and all sources for the past three (3) years.
   b. In addition to the documents provided in a., please produce any statements, projections, estimates and any other documents prepared and/or provided to you evidencing any commissions, bonuses, and income you may receive in the foreseeable future.

2. PERSONAL TAX RETURNS
   a. Please produce complete copies of any and all income tax returns filed by you, individually and/or jointly with any other person(s), with the federal and state governments for the past five (5) years. If the filing date of any return has been delayed and/or extended, identify the return and produce a copy of any extension and your payment of estimated taxes.
   b. All W-4 forms that have been given to your employer since your date of original employment.

3. CHECKING/SAVINGS/BANKING AND OTHER CASH ACCOUNTS STATEMENTS
   a. Please provide all records of bank checking accounts, savings accounts, credit union accounts, and investment and money market accounts maintained by you, individually and/or jointly with other person(s), including, but not limited to, monthly bank statements, canceled checks, deposit slips, check registers, statements relating to savings accounts, certificates of deposit, and any other such records from January 1, 201__ to the date of trial of this case.
   b. If you have signing authority on any banking, checking, or other account, but the account is maintained in the name of another person or entity, produce all listed records for said account for the same period above.

4. CREDIT CARD STATEMENTS

Any and all monthly credit card and revolving charge card statements and receipts showing all charges and payments made and the balance due on any credit cards or charge accounts of any kind, maintained by you or regularly used by you.

This request includes any accounts maintained in your name, jointly with any person(s), or the name of your employer or any other person or entity who provides a credit card for your use, for the period from January 1, 20__ to the date of trial in this action.

5. COMPENSATION AGREEMENTS, EMPLOYMENT CONTRACTS AND RELATED EMPLOYMENT INFORMATION

Produce any and all agreements, letters, employment contracts, and/or information you received from your present employer relating to your compensation including, but not limited to: documents evidencing or explaining salary, bonuses, commissions, pay raises, promotions, payroll deductions, advances, deferred compensation, retirement benefits, stock options, or other benefits arising from or relating to your employment, which you are or were entitled from the time you first became employed to the hearing date in this trial.

6. INVESTIGATIONS

Provide any and all investigative/detective reports, and related agreements, invoices, photographs, film, tape recordings, audio recordings, and other tangible evidence and information of any nature relating to or arising from any surveillance or investigation of the conduct, activities, or behavior of the parties in this case, which surveillance or investigation was performed on your behalf in connection with this action.

7. TANGIBLE EVIDENCE

Produce any and all tangible evidence of any nature that is in the possession or control of you or your attorney, or which is being held for you by any person or entity for safe keeping, which evidence relates, in any manner, to the conduct of the parties in this action, including, but not limited to: notes, cards, letters, photographs, film, pictures, screenshots, printouts, invoices, billing records, documents, tapes, voice recordings, audio recordings, clothes, or any other tangible evidence of any nature.

8. BUDGET

Please provide your required financial disclosure affidavit that you intend to present at any hearing or trial in this action.

9. DOCUMENTARY EVIDENCE

If you have any financial documents of any type or any other documentary evidence relevant to this action, which evidence may be used in trial, but which has not otherwise been requested in these numbered paragraphs, please produce such evidence.

10. LAWSUITS/LEGAL PROCEEDINGS

Provide any and all true copies of any and all civil complaints/petitions, answers, applications, motions, responses, discovery, and all other pleadings with respect to any and all lawsuits or legal proceedings now pending or pending at any time within the past five years in which you are/were a party or in which you or any of your property has been or could have been affected, including without limitation, all pleadings with respect to any garnishment, attachment(s), and/or foreclosure proceedings within the past five (5) years.

11. EXPERTS

Please identify each and every individual you may call as an expert witness at any trial and/or hearing in this case, and for each individual so identified, please state:

a. the subject matter which the expert is expected to testify;
b. the substance of the facts and opinions to which the expert is expected to testify; and
c. a summary of the grounds for each opinion
d. Any dates and times you met with said expert witness
e. Any payments made by you and/or on your behalf to said individual.

12. CHILD SUPPORT CALCULATIONS

Provide all child support calculator worksheets (whether the original worksheet and/or amended versions) prepared by you and/or your attorney that you intend to use at any hearing or trial in the above-styled action, including, but not limited to, any such worksheets you have prepared in connection with the pending matter or any other matter in the last five years whether in this State or elsewhere.

13. CRIMINAL CHARGES

Produce any and all documents related to any criminal charges and/or serious traffic charges filed against you in this State or in any other jurisdiction, whether or not they resulted in convictions, for the past ten (10) years. Please do not submit any minor traffic infractions (speeding tickets, running a stop sign, etc.).

14. PROTECTIVE ORDERS

All documents related to any peace order/restraining orders or protective order cases filed by you or against you, in this State or in any other jurisdiction, in the past ten (10) years.

15. SUBSTANCE ABUSE/MENTAL HEALTH TREATMENT

Produce any and all documents related to any substance abuse and/or mental health (including therapy, counseling, and/or psychiatric) treatment you have undergone in the past ten (10) years, including, but not limited to, inpatient treatment and outpatient treatment, name of any treating physician, and dates you attended said treatment.

16. CHILDCARE RECORDS

Produce any and all records you have of the child's school (public and private), pre-K, babysitting, or daycare, including any attendance records if the child was present at any daycare or childcare or had a babysitter and the cost of said care and including proof of payment.

17. CHILD'S MEDICAL RECORDS

Produce any and all medical records of the minor child in this case that are in your possession. This request includes dental, vision, pediatric, therapy notes, and all other medical records relating to the child(ren) in this action.

18. CHILD'S MEDICATION RECORDS
Produce any and all pharmacy records or other evidence of any medications the child takes, including the name of the medication, the dosage, the physician who prescribed the medication, and for what condition the medication is prescribed.

19. PROOF OF AUTOMOBILE INSURANCE AND DRIVER'S LICENSE
A copy of your current driver's license and proof of automobile liability insurance on any vehicle the child(ren) in this action is transported.

Index

A
ABA Model Rule 1.2(c), 14
ABA Model Rule 4.3, 58
Accuity, 26
AdobeSign, 26
alcohol usage, 43, 118
alternative compensation agreements (ACAs), 10–14
  benefits of, 11–12
  flat fees, 13
  overview of, 10–11
  subscription fee arrangement, 13–14
American Academy of Matrimonial Lawyers, 53
American Psychiatric Association (APA), 43
App Close, 23
Association of Family and Conciliation Courts, 66
Atlanta Legal Aid Society, 5
audio, for video trials, 98–99
automate document generation, 23

B
best interest of the child standard, 42, 70, 90
billing models, 9–19. *See also* alternative compensation agreements (ACAs); retainers
blogs, 43
boilerplate language requirements, 29
BookMe, 26
budget, 22, 64, 123

C
capped hour arrangement, 14–15
case management software, 7, 18, 22, 30
  client alerts and, 7
  client portal on, 22
  integrating with CRM software, 28
  well-known, 22
  workflow tracker/deadline trackers and, 30
certified criminal convictions, 41–42
"cheat sheet" of counselors, 3
childcare facilities, 40
childcare records, 40, 124
child custody litigation
  Child Custody Case Intake Form, 110–114
  commonly requested documents in, 109
  in COVID-19 pandemic, 97–101
  interrogatories sample, 118–119
  mediation and, 76
  online intake forms, 27
  "Petition for Modification of Custody," 23
  Request for Production of Documents for Child Custody Cases, 120–125
  sample engagement letter for contested child custody matter, 106–108

child support
calculations, 29, 124
demonstrative exhibits for, 94–95
health insurance coverage, 79
interrogatories and, 49
land records and, 36
mediation, 78–79
non-disparagement and, 78
in opening statement, 92
prior actions, 36
salaries for, Labor Statistics on, 36
splitting costs, 78–79
stipulation for, 88
suppressing income to minimize, 42
client
documents retrieved by, 6
home of, pictures of, 6
in mental health therapy, 65–66, 69
preparing for trial, 88–89
psychological counseling for, 2–4, 106
responsiveness of, 7–8
story of, 5–6
client alerts, 7
client journal, 37–38
client portals, 22
closings, 91–92
cloud storage, 25
composition notebooks, 38
consultation with expert, 66–67
coParenter, 23, 24
co-parenting
interrogatories and, 49
parenting coordinator and, 70
right of first refusal, 77
software for, 23–24, 29
Coparently, 23
cost
assessing, at court, 66
cost-saving tips, 1, 4, 6, 38
of depositions, 83
of experts, 64–65, 66
of factual development, 33–46
cost-effective trial, 87–95
demonstrative exhibits, 94–95
evidence, 92
legal financing options, 87
objections, 92
openings and closings, 91–92
post judgment, 95
preparing your client, 88–89
pretrial motions, 89–90
pretrial statement/order, 89
settlement during trial, 93–95
stipulations, 87–88
supplementary discovery, 92
before trial, 87–90
during trial, 90–93
unnecessary witnesses, 90–91
court-appointed experts, 64, 67–68
court-mandated remote hearings, 31
COVID-19 pandemic
court-mandated remote hearings, 31
litigating child custody in, 97–101
See also video trials
credibility, 47, 50–51, 62
credit card processing, 27
crime statistics for area of parent's residence, 41, 46
criminal charges/convictions, 41–42
cross-examination
alcohol abuse of other parent and, 51
depositions and, 83
education records and, 39
exhibits in, 100
housing instability of other parent and, 44
instructional testimony and, 65
physical/mental health of other parent and, 43, 69
preparing client for, 89
religious institutions and, 40
social media and, 43
stipulations and, 88
treatises for, 66
of unnecessary witnesses, 90
Custodian of the Records Certificate, 39
Custody X Change, 29
customer relationship management (CRM) software, 27–28

D

dating apps, 54
deadline tracker, 30

Department of Family and Children Services
records, 45
subpoena, 115–117
depositions, 81–86
applicable rules for, 84
to avoid surprises at trial, 82
cons of conducting, 83–84
cost of, 83
documents for, 85
exhibits for, 85
information revealed to other side in, 83
investigations and, 85–86
Notice of Deposition, 84
opposing counsel in, evaluating, 82
opposing counsel in, opening the door for, 84
opposing counsel in, unprofessional, 86
outline for, 85–86
preserving and locking in testimony, 81
pros of conducting, 81–82
settlement and, 82
spontaneous responses in, 82
trial runs and, 83
unknown witnesses identified in, 84
video, 83
witnesses in, evaluating, 82
Diagnostic and Statistical Manual of Mental Disorders (DSM-5), 43
direct examination, 6, 39, 65, 66
directories for finding experts, 65
discovery, 47–55
interrogatories, 48–49
preparing responses, 30–31
public profiles and internet searches, 54–55
public records in, 34
Requests for Admissions of Fact (RFAs), 49–51
Requests for Production of Documents, 51–52
social media data in, 42–43, 53–54
subpoenas, 55
supplementary, 92
text messages, phone logs, and photographs taken on phones, 24–25
tools of, 47–51
docket search, 40, 42
documentary evidence, 123
documents
automate document generation, 23
client's retrieval of, 6
commonly requested documents list in child custody litigation, 109
for depositions, 85
Request for Production of Documents for Child Custody Cases, 120–125
subpoena for production of (*see* subpoenas)
DocuSign, 26
Domestic Relations Interrogatories form, 48
domestic violence
disclosure of a party's address and, 77
history of, in new significant other, 42
interrogatories, 49
parenting coordinator and, 70–71
photographs taken of injuries in, 25
settlement during trial and, 93
driver's license, 125
Droid Transfer, 24
drug test, 83
drug usage, 43, 83, 84, 118

E
EasySoft, 29
education records, 38–39
electronic client journal, 37
electronic copy of Facebook data, 53
electronic expert directory, 65
electronic filing, 99–100
electronic signature, 26
electronic signing software, 25–26
engagement letter
for contested child custody matter, sample of, 106–108
costs spelled out in, 10, 13–14, 17
Psychological/Counseling provision in, 3
signing, 2, 26
E-Sign Genie, 26
evergreen retainer, 15

evidence. *See* discovery; factual development
exhibits
  for cost-effective trial, 94–95
  delivering, 100
  for depositions, 85
  for video trials, 99–100
experts, 63–73
  child's school counselor, 72–73
  consultation with, 66–67
  cost of, assessing, 66
  court-appointed, 67–68
  directories for finding, 65
  flat fee for, 64–65
  identifying, 124
  for instructional testimony, 65
  juvenile court referral, 71–72
  mental health, 68–69
  need for, determining, 63–64
  parenting coordinator, 70–71
  parent's therapist as, 65–66
  private investigator, 69–70
  references of, 67, 68
  shopping for, 64
  stipulations for, 67
  treatises as, 66
extracurricular activities, 78
extracurricular activities, evidence of available, 44–45

F
Facebook, 53–54
factual development, 33–46
  certified criminal convictions, 41–42
  childcare facilities, 40
  client journal, 37–38
  crime rates and other information for area of parent's residence, 41
  Department of Family & Children Services records, 45
  docket search for opposing party's new significant other, 42
  education records, 38–39
  extracurricular activities, evidence of, 44–45
  international relocation matters, 45–46
  Labor Statistics on salaries for child support, 36
  land records, 36–37
  needs of minor child, 44
  other parent's instability of housing, 44
  other public resources, 35
  physical/mental health of other parent, 43
  prior orders regarding same parties, 35–36
  public records, 34–35
  religious institutions, 40
  school ratings, 39
  social media of all parties, 42–43
Family Law Software, 29
Federal Poverty Guidelines, 16
Federal Rules of Evidence Rule 612, 37
financial disclosure affidavit, 5, 29–30, 33
financial records, 55, 94–95
flat fees
  for experts, 64–65
  phased, 13
  retainer combined with, 17–18
  subscription fee arrangement, 13–14
  triggering events and, 13, 17–18
form interrogatories, 48–49

G
ghost attorney service, 13–14
goals, 4
Google Calendar, 26
Google Forms, 27
Google Maps, 24
Google searches, 53, 54–55
G-Suite, 27
Guardian Ad Litem, 7, 12, 61, 63, 71

H
health insurance coverage, 79
Health Insurance Portability and Accountability Act (HIPAA), 55
hearsay exceptions, 34
HelloSign, 26
"he said/she said" disputes, 24, 51
hidden vault searches, 54

holidays, 76–77
home
of client, pictures of, 6
crime rates and other information for area of, 41
other parent's instability of housing, 44
homeschooled child, 39

I
iBackup Viewer, 24
individualized education program (IEP), 44
initial consultation, 1–8, 16, 26, 27, 28
documents retrieved by client, 6
goals, 4
home of client, pictures of, 6
meeting questions, 7
plan, devising, 7
psychological counseling, 2–4
responsiveness of client, 7–8
right to withdrawal, 4–5
story of client, 5–6
tone, setting, 2
initial pleadings, 2, 48
instructional testimony, experts for, 65
insurance coverage
automobile, 125
health, 79, 88
intake forms
online, 27
sample of, 110–114
Internal Revenue Service, 52
international relocation matters, 45–46
internet access, video trials and, 98
internet searches for evidence, 54–55
interrogatories, 48–49
credibility and, 50
form interrogatories, 48–49
reviewing and revising, 52
sample of, 118–119
spontaneous responses and, 82
investigations, for depositions, 85–86
iPhone log, 24

J
juvenile court referral, 71–72

K
Kids First!, 29

L
Labor Statistics on salaries for child support, 36
land records, 36–37
lawsuits or legal proceedings, pending, 123
LawTap, 26
legal custody, 76
legal financing options, 87
legal jargon, 59–60
Lincoln, Abraham, 9
low bono appeals resources, 18, 95

M
marital estate finances, software to manage, 29–30
mediation, 75–79
access to school and medical records, 79
establishing bottom line, 76–79
extracurricular activities, 78
health insurance coverage, 79
holidays, 76–77
legal custody, 76
meeting beforehand, 75–76
non-disparagement, 77–78
relocation, 77
right of first refusal, 77
support issues, 78–79
medical records/bills, 6, 55, 79, 124, 125
mental health
apps, 31–32
client already be in therapy for, 65–66, 69
DSM-5 and, 43
experts, 68–69
interrogatories and, 49
of minor child, 44, 69
of other parent, 43
records, 55, 124
messaging apps, 54
microphone, for video trials, 98–99
Microsoft Excel spreadsheets, 95

Microsoft Office, 30
Microsoft Sticky Notes, 30
Mosten, Forrest S., 14
Motion to Appoint a Guardian Ad Litem, 7

N
needs of minor child, 44
new significant other, docket search for opposing party's, 42
911 reports and call transcripts or recordings, 35
non-disparagement, 77–78
no-shows, 24, 26
Notice of Deposition, 84
Notice of Records Deposition, 55

O
objections, 92
office
  atmosphere, 2
  chair, 99
  cleanliness of, 31
online calendaring/booking software, 26
online intake forms, 27
open-ended questions, 2
openings and closings, 91–92
opposing counsel
  evaluating, 82
  information revealed to, 83
  Notice of Deposition, 84
  unprofessional, 86
Our Family Wizard, 23, 24
Outlook
  calendar, 26
  letter templates, 30

P
pandemic technology, 97–101. *See also* video trials
parenting coordinator, 70–71
parenting time
  on Child Custody Case Intake Form, 114
  items/clothing not returned from, 38
  plan, 5, 40
  religious institution and, 40
  software, 28–29
PartUs, 29
payment apps, 54
PDF-to-Word converter, 30
"Petition for Modification of Custody," 23
phased flat fee, 13
phone call log, 24–25, 52
phone call log backup software, 24–25
phone logs, 24–25
photographs taken on phones, 24–25, 52
physical health of other parent, 43
PickTime, 26
post judgment, 95
preparing your client, 88–89
pretrial motions, 89–90
pretrial statement/order, 89
prior orders regarding parties, 35–36
private investigator, 69–70
pro bono services, 4, 18, 95
pro se litigants, 57–62
  avoiding legal jargon with, 59–60
  explaining your actions to, 59
  overview of, 57
  remaining professional with, 59
  resolving issues with, 60–61
  risks of negotiating with, 61–62
  seeking judge's assistance with, 60
  stating your role to, 58
  taking seriously, 61
protective orders, 36, 93, 117, 124
psychological counseling, 2–4, 106
Psychological/Counseling provision, 3
public auction records, 55
public profiles, 54–55
public records, 34–35
public resources, other, 35

Q
questions
  in discovery, 47–48
  expert consultation and, 67
  in first consultation, 2

interrogatories, 48–49
meeting, 7
in mock interviews, 68
open-ended, 2
preparing client for, 88
from *pro se* opponent, 58
spontaneous answers to, 82

R

Reagan, Ronald, 41
records
access to school and medical, 79
childcare, 40, 124
Department of Family & Children Services, 45
education, 38–39
financial, 55, 94–95
homeschooled child, 39
land, 36–37
medical, 6, 55, 79, 124, 125
mental health, 55, 124
public, 34–35
public auction, 55
subpoenas for (*see* subpoenas)
tax, 52
referrals
to juvenile court, 71–72
to potential clients, 28, 64
religious institutions, 40
relocation, 77
remote hearings, court-mandated, 31. *See also* video trials
Request for Production of Documents for Child Custody Cases, 120–125
residence. *See* home
resource counselor, 4
retainers, 14–19
capped hour arrangement, 14–15
combination of flat fee and retainer, 17–18
evergreen retainer, 15
language provision in, 5
sliding fee scales billable hours, 16
right of first refusal, 77
right to withdrawal, 4–5
Rules of Evidence as a Writing Used to Refresh a Witness's Recollection, 37

S

school counselors, 72–73
school ratings, 39
Scully, Elizabeth Potter, 14
SetMore, 26
settlement during trial, 93–95
sex offender registry, 41
SignEasy, 26
sliding fee, 16
SMS Backup+, 24
social media, 42–43
apps, 54
in discovery, 53–54
Facebook, 53–54
in factual development, 42–43
public profiles, 54–55
for witness's background for depositions, 85
Social Security Earnings Histories, 52
software
case management (*see* case management software)
co-parenting, 23–24
customer relationship management (CRM), 27–28
customer service of, 97–98
electronic signing, 25–26
hacks, 30–31
to manage finances of marital estate, 29–30
online calendaring/booking, 26
parenting time, 28–29
text message/phone call log backup, 24–25, 52
video conferencing, 31, 97
See also technology
stipulations
deposition, 84
for experts, 67
in supplement discovery, 92
before trial, 87–88, 89
story of the client, 5–6
subpoenas
for child's counselor, 72–73
cost of serving, 83
for Custodian of the Records Certificate, 39

subpoenas (*continued*)
Department of Family and Children Services, 45, 115–117
in discovery, 48
for education records, 38, 39
Notice of Records Deposition, 55
for public records, 34, 35
for unnecessary witnesses, 91
subscription fee arrangement, 13–14
substance abuse, 49, 68, 69, 124
supplementary discovery, 92
surprises at trial, avoiding, 82

T
Talking Parents, 23
tax records, 52
technology, 21–32
automate document generation, 23
cloud storage, 25
court-mandated remote hearings, 31
credit card processing, 27
financial disclosure affidavit automation, 29–30
mental health apps, 31–32
online intake forms, 27
pandemic, 97–101 (*see also* video trials)
workflow tracker and deadline trackers, 30
See also software
text messages, 24–25, 52
themes, 2, 6, 30, 85, 91–92
therapist as experts, 65–66
tone, setting, 2
ToneMeter™, 24
treatises, 66
trial, cost-effective. *See* cost-effective trial
trial runs, 83

U
Unbundled Legal Services: A Family Lawyer's Guide (Mosten and Scully), 14
United States Bureau of Labor Statistics, 36
unknown witnesses, 84
unprofessional opposing counsel and, dealing with, 86
unrepresented opposing party. *See* *pro se* litigants

V
video conferencing software, 31, 97
video depositions, 83
video doorbells, 54
video trials
backup internet access, 98
etiquette for, 99
exhibits for, 99–100
home office chair for, 99
microphone and audio, 98–99
shortcomings of, warnings of, 100–101
webcams, 98
Virginia Code § 16.1-244, 72

W
webcams, 98
witnesses
deposition of, 82
evaluating, 82
expert (*see* experts)
investigation of, 85
unknown, 84
unnecessary, 90–91
workflow tracker, 30